TO:

Doug

Lanier speaks
very highly of you !!!
That's good enough
         for me !!!

Enjoy!

Jerry Brown

IRRITABLE BOWELS AND THE PEOPLE WHO GIVE YOU THEM

IRRITABLE BOWELS
AND THE PEOPLE
WHO GIVE YOU THEM

TERRY SWEENEY

DUKE STREET PRESS
Boston New York London

FIRST EDITION

Library of Congress Control Number: 2015906459

Duke Street Press
Beaufort, South Carolina

ISBN: 978-0-692-43444-4

Cover designed by Hope A. Falls

DEDICATION

I know this is normally where authors write some heartfelt paean to their extraordinary parents, thanking them for their most memorable contribution to their lives. Flowery tributes like... To my father who told me when I was just a child "Your words have the power to feed minds and fill hearts." Or...To my mother who once said to me, "The world is a garden just waiting for you to flower." But I'm having a tough time of it. What inspiring bon mots did my folks ever spout when I was down in the dumps and needed a poetic piece of parental wisdom to lift me up? I racked my brain. Well, long ago when I was brooding about not getting elected President of the Chess Club in eighth grade, my father did say, "Sonny boy, I've got one thing to tell you about this world... it stinks." Unfortunately, that didn't help then and it doesn't help now.

Maybe my mother... She must have said something I carry with me to this day. Wait a minute... Once when my mother was driving over some bumpy railroad tracks without slowing down and my father who was in the car had yelped, "Jeez, Lenore!" My mother did turn to me in the back seat and shout, "Your father's got a fairy's ass." Okay, not exactly Shakespeare. But it did stay with me. Later in life when I discovered I had a 'fairy's ass' of my own, it was a great comfort to know who I got it from.

Contents

Introduction
by Pat Conroy

Humor has always been the darkest god of art. Pity the poor comedians of the world, the ones who make you scream with laughter, who leave you weightless with a pure spirit of joy, and whom you clamor to see when your life goes routine and driftless and unbearable to you. Standup comedy reigns supreme on as the most difficult callisthenic and the most dangerous high wire act in the acting profession. Behind every joke is a tragedy. The best laughs always come from the saddest clown in the circus. It's as difficult a way to make a living as being an astronaut or an avatar of a new religion. As I write this, the French cartoonists at Charlie Hebdo lie dead in their graves around France for the mortal sin of being funny. Ten thousand hilarious men and women will arise to take their place. Humor is the only thing that can save the world from the overdose of seriousness that has always been an ineradicable plague wherever our species finds itself. Our comedians serve as the warrior tribe who alert us to madness and folly and all the killings zones of stupidity itself.

Terry Sweeney is the funniest man I ever met and he has written one of the most hilarious books I've ever read. I first heard of Terry and his work on *Saturday Night Live* from my children and my great friend Doug Marlette. He told me that Terry's imitation of Nancy Reagan was comedy at its finest and acting in its highest form. Doug had taped all the episodes of *Saturday Night Live* and forced me to watch Terry Sweeney perform his brilliant sendup of the First Lady. Doug and I spent the day laughing at every word or gesture or facial expression Terry made. In discovering his brilliance, I learned something about the best comedy from Terry's knockout performance. He did nothing to make me loathe or condescend to Mrs. Reagan and in fact, the opposite happened. He opened the First Lady to my understanding and I could feel the tenderness and respect that the comedian felt for his subject. It's what all great actors do. When they play a part, and have that portion of genius and humanity to summon at their will, they can open up a historical or fictional character like a rose window on their character. I never thought much about Nancy Reagan until Terry Sweeney brought her to immemorial life. The same thing happened when I saw Amy Poehler play Hillary Clinton, Tina Fey play Sarah Palin, and Will Ferrell play George W. Bush.

Terry Sweeney and his spouse Lanier Laney moved to Beaufort, South Carolina in 2007. Lanier had been a staff writer for *Saturday Night Live* and together they had co-written the classic Carolina beach movie *Shag*. This brought them into my life and I often wondered why an openly gay married couple would choose Beaufort, a southern town of ten thousand southern-fried and often illiberal souls, after leaving the bright lights of Manhattan or the harsh sunlight of Hollywood. *Irritable Bowels and the People Who Give You Them* will tell you the story with humor, irreverence, insight, surprise and even savagery. Terry's savage eye is my favorite thing about him. In this book's insider's guide to why you should stick your head in an oven if you ever find yourself dreaming of becoming an actor, a comedian, or, god forbid, a writer, he leaves no tombstone unturned. I had thought I had a nightmarish story of an agent's meeting in Hollywood. Terry's story makes me want to give the entire state of California back to Mexico. In this book, which has led to my both hating and loving all living things, Terry relates the tale of lunch in a shi-shi, tofu-infused, Cobb Salad souled restaurant in Santa Monica, that will make readers not want to eat lunch for a year.

The chapter "Fifty Shades of Cherokee" is one of the most hilarious things I've ever read in English. I would call it a small masterpiece, except I think it is a work of comic art worthy of Dickens or Twain or Woody Allen. Because I'm introducing this book, I want to blurt out all these stories – these rich, divine, fall on your knees laughing stories. He combines the novelist's cunning eye with the wordsmith's brilliant turn of phrase with the born comic's sense of deadly timing. I screamed laughing while reading this wonderful book. I can't imagine being an actor, comedian, screenwriter or author and not wanting to read this book. It's like a cannibal telling jokes to the poor schnook he's about to have for dinner.

To all the readers of this book, I advise you to steal these stories and pretend they are yours. Tell them at dinner parties and family reunions, especially if you don't want to be invited to a dinner party again in your life or don't mind seeing your name expunged from any will that might mention you as an heir. This book is profane, but profane is way too sweet a word to describe it. Try outrageous. Try fabulous.

Because I adore Terry Sweeney, after reading this book I gave him a lifetime supply of Metamucil and free colonoscopies for the rest of his life.

Then I told him he was a national treasure.

Pat Conroy

Irritable Bowels and The People Who Give You Them

Big Italian families just love to pigeonhole everybody's kids including their own. And once neatly labeled; they will perpetuate their amateur snap judgments in a lazy man's shorthand. "Oh she's the smart one..." "He's the athletic one..." "This one's the pretty one..." and "That one's the sneaky one..." and so you are identified for life. My poor cousin who was born with a slight birth defect, which required her to wear a special shoe for a short time, was referred to in my mother's family (even after she had completed a Doctorate and a Ph.D. in Quantum Physics) as "the one with the bum foot." So bear with me as I try to set the record straight. You see, I was misclassified by my relatives as... "the one with the nervous bowels."

Okay so I was a colicky infant. I was most likely allergic to something in the crappy formula they were peddling at the time to mothers whom they'd shamed into not breastfeeding. So, of course, there were baby cramps down there and red–faced crying fits that went on for months. And yes, later; as a young child; I may have suffered an unexpected bowel disturbance or two caused by something I ate but my relatives never let me forget it. My Aunt Emma warned me at my college graduation homecoming dinner at her house"...be careful this eggplant's spicy... but don't worry, I gave you an old padded chair, that I don't care what happens to, in case you have an accident." Jesus God! What humiliation. I was absolutely fine. As a matter of fact, as I grew up and thought back on the meals I'd shared with my immediate family; it began to dawn on me that maybe the real problem had always been not what I was eating but who I was eating with.

I don't know what rituals you and your family had around the dinner table, but in my family as soon as the meal was served and my mother sat down to join my father, my older brother and myself; everybody savagely dug in like the starving winners of a reward challenge on an episode of 'Survivor'. Everybody except me; before starting in on my food, I would loudly pray "Thank you Lord for what we are about to receive"... hoping in vain to shame the heathens around me. Then ignoring them, my own private mealtime ritual would begin. I would dramatically bend over my plate, my thick dorky glasses steaming up and reverently sniff each and every item on it. The fresh pungent garlic my Italian mother had rubbed on the London broil mixed with the savory meaty beef juices. Next to it, I inhaled the glorious aroma of salt and melting butter on a fluffy baked potato whose charred earthy skin whisked me outdoors where the sweet smell of fresh-picked peas on my plate from my mother's garden danced around my head. I was floating on an aromatic cloud in Foodie Heaven.

But the sound of my dear sweet mother's voice would bring me back to earth. "FOR CHRIST'S SAKE, WHAT THE HELL ARE YOU DOING?!! THERE IS NOTHING WRONG WITH YOUR FOOD!!!" "Maybe four-eyes needs stronger glasses," my jerky older brother was only too happy to volunteer.

"Shut up, stupid!" my father would yell at my brother, which would prompt my mother to scream. "Don't you dare call him stupid! Even if he is!... which would then cause my brother to shout, "This is all your fault!" then slug me, which prompted me to throw my milk in his face and then the usual nightly all out screaming, slapping melee would erupt. And before my bowels knew what hit 'em, they were once again on the mat down for the count. Can you blame them?

As soon as I got out of that house, off to college and then afterwards on my own... Surprise! No problem whatsoever downstairs in the old Willie Wonka Chocolate Factory! Everybody on the assembly line was humming along happily doing their job. It wasn't till I arrived in Hollywood that I encountered digestive challenges once more; and faced the evil Bowel Bogeyman in one of his most cleverly camouflaged hiding places: the Business Lunch.

The Hollywood business lunch is like one of those beautiful Sirens in 'Ulysses' whose sweet song lured innocent sailors to their doom. First of all... it's free...yippee... somebody else is paying for a fancy pants lunch in a fabulous restaurant you could never afford. Secondly, it could help your career... The agent/executive producer/network suit who's fronting the bill might just drop a juicy job opportunity in your lap. This is your chance to get some one on one quality time with Mr. or Ms. Big shot. Thirdly you'll most likely be seen by others at one of these chic industry watering holes. Who knows who'll pass you their card or better yet remember you the next time they've got an available writing or acting gig? They'll see you. They'll remember you. They'll hire you. It sure sounds like Win-Win-Win, doesn't it? Tell that to my bowels. They know better...

The Business Lunch with My Agent

My agent has the delightful habit of chewing with his mouth open while still insisting on talking non-stop about show business. I can tell you most assuredly that the sight of soggy, mushy half-eaten food in the flapping jaws of this man is enough to begin the slow queasy shutdown of my inner food processor. Call me crazy, but it also doesn't help my digestion when someone's going on and on about some other writers' opening weekend box office grosses whose movies just made God knows how many millions when I had to search the cushions of my couch for loose change to buy gas to get there to meet 'em. Spitting egg salad in my face, he'll gleefully inform me that some rival agent's client's romantic comedy just tanked. "Romantic comedy is dead. DEAD! Nobody wants to see 'em and nobody wants to make 'em!!!" Apparently forgetting, *I'm* writing a romantic comedy on spec because *he told* me to …at our last business lunch six months ago. I can't believe my ears. Down boy...I tell the pit bull in my belly that's now growling. My agent then insists I order dessert. He's unfortunately getting a wedge of cherry cheesecake... I can only imagine what that's going to look like stuck in his teeth. I make myself order a simple bland crème brûlée so I'll have something to look down at instead of his cherry cheese–filled mouth of horrors.

When dessert arrives, I take my spoon and pretend to slide it into my lush, creamy custard. To tell the truth, it looks so good I'm very tempted to give it a try. It's right then that my agent says "Sorry to rush you... but I just realized I've got an appointment in fifteen minutes to have my back waxed." Oh, dear God. The vision of his hairy back now fills my head. I return my dessert spoon to the table unused. He quickly shovels a large white and red gob of cherry cheese goo into his mouth. What happens next isn't pretty. I pretend to cough into my napkin, although it's really more a gag than a cough.

I'm reminded that this isn't the first business lunch where someone shared intimate personal health and grooming info once rightly considered off-limits 'au table' in polite conversation. I've had to hear about mere passing business acquaintance's colonics, herpes outbreaks and yeast infections ad nauseam. No really. I felt nauseam. Shopping for my groceries in Hollywood supermarkets; I have seen more than one outpatient fresh from their plastic surgeon's office blithely strolling down the dairy aisle with a ghoulish, acid-peeled face with matching hideous swollen collagen fish lips. Whatever happened to sending a friend to the store? "Mary Lou... I look like a med-school cadaver right now; could you pick me up a quart of milk?"

Blessedly this lunch ends quickly, and I pretend to take my to-go box home. "Let's do this again, soon..." he yells over his shoulder. Sadly, I know I will. I'll have to. You can't say no to a business lunch with your agent. Not in this town.

There is still yet another hideous form of business lunch. It's when busy Hollywood producers in a hurry want to hear your idea while they eat because... duh... they're busy. Of course, I'm always nervous. It could mean a boat load of much needed money, if they say yes. But pitching to high-powered executives over food is something "the one with the nervous bowels" HATES...

The Business Lunch Pitch

Two women producers at the Lifetime Network have called my agent and specifically requested me. It's for a T.V. Movie about a novice woman firefighter who faces prejudice and hostile we-don't-want-you-here-lady chauvinism when she joins an all-male firehouse. It's based on a true story. I read and re-read the quite serious article in Ms. Magazine that it's based on. Calling *me*... a comedy writer... can only mean one thing... they want me to bring the funny to this lunch. Okay... hold on to your Cobb salads, ladies. Here I come.

When I walk into the swanky Beverly Hills eatery; two women at a corner table wave me over. Nancy and Rita, the two Lifetime execs jump up and greet me effusively like I'm a literary giant whom they have idolized for years. "We're big fans of your work," gushes Nancy. "Me too!" I gush back. We all laugh uproariously. Well, whaddaya' know? My business lunch is off to a great start. "What are you working on now?" gasps Rita excitedly. "I really can't say," I announce with a mysterious smile. I really can't–cuz I'm not working on a damn thing. I'm broke again and I just turned 40. In Hollywood, that's the age you start shopping around for a special ring to hold your cyanide capsule. "Let's order right away! I can't wait to hear your ideas!" whispers Nancy excitedly. As I predicted, it's Cobb salads all around. I'm so relaxed I think I just may actually eat mine.

While we wait for our food, I launch into my little spiel about how I've studied the magazine article they optioned for the movie and understand completely how they would need someone like me to punch it up. "Let me level with you, ladies; there's not one laugh in this thing so far." The two of them look at each other alarmed. "I know that's hard to hear, but the good news is I've already got some easy fixes." With that I jump right in "I say we go a little wild here. What if she's a dancer in a cheesy men's bar? You know, a single mother who got pregnant in high school, now struggling to support herself and the kid. She's tired of her down and dirty life and wants to trade in her stripper pole for a pole in a firehouse. We could call it 'A Change of Hose'."

The two stare at me speechless as I pause to sip my iced tea that's just been delivered. The caffeine really hits me fast and I feel like I'm on a roll. "Now, if we really wanna jump on the crazy train, I say we make her a prostitute with a heart of gold who's always had this one dream... to fight fires. We call it... "Hooker and Ladder." Now does that scream ratings or what?" At this point, Nancy narrows her eyes and leans forward menacingly. "Are you the Terrence Sweeney who wrote 'Shadow of Guilt'?" "Uh, no." I answer, taken aback. Rita jumps in– "The Prodigal Father?" I shake my head no. "So I guess it's safe to assume you didn't write 'I Want to Die' either?" asks Nancy sourly. "Not unless it's die laughing," I offer up with a shaky laugh of my own. They are not amused.

A joyless lead balloon has landed with a thud on the snow-white silent tablecloth. Our three lunch salads arrive right on cue. "Enjoy!" chirps our cheery gay waiter as he obliviously sashays off to get us more iced tea... I slowly and stiffly make myself stand up like in one of those home-from-the-war movies where the protagonist is trying out his prosthetic legs for the first time to see if they work. "I'm guessing I'm the wrong Terrence Sweeney... I'm just going to go now; if that's alright..." Nancy rolls her eyes and shrugs as if to say 'don't think either one of us is going to stop you.' I tiptoe as quickly as possible to the door of the restaurant never looking back at my not-so-long-ago two biggest fans. As I reach for the door I hear Rita say on her mobile phone to her assistant... "Adrienne, you really fucked up this time."

Two weeks later, I am accidentally introduced at a party to the other Terrence Sweeney. He's a former Catholic priest (now a serious Emmy-winning writer here in Hollywood). I tell him about my mix-up. He tells me he used to run into former parishioners who had heard he ended up on Saturday Night Live doing drag.

They'd been praying for him ever since. We both laugh and for the first time since that ill-fated business lunch, my gut relaxes. No more pitching over lunch ever again for me. Or so I swear. But it is the next category of business lunch... that well... marks the end of Hollywood business lunches for me, once and for all...

THE SEE AND BE SEEN BUSINESS LUNCH

My friend, Eva, calls and invites me to lunch with her at the trendy restaurant du jour in Santa Monica where all the Hollywood movers and shakers are currently chowing down. Eva's a tough-talking Cuban spitfire who handles all the big movie and T.V. ads for the New York Times. She's a top executive with an expense account that was created solely to schmooze studio big wigs over impressive, free business lunches. Somebody's canceled so she calls me... "You know I don't like mixing eating and show business, Eva." "Hey, asshole, this isn't Hollywood calling. This is me, your friend. Put on a fresh pair of panties and get over here...now."

Once there, Eva greets me with an already poured glass of expensive cabernet. "God, I hate this place," she gripes. "It's fucking crawling with stars." I feel a certain tightening in my belly immediately after that remark but the red wine soothingly reassures my gut that all is well. I bury my head in the menu and study the overly self-conscious, astronomically-priced offerings of biodynamic, hand-raised micro greens and obscure organic ragouts of Moroccan whooziwhat over quinoa. These esoteric menus make me nervous... What to order? Never mind- Eva, who has bigger balls than most guys I know, has already taken over. She always knows exactly what she wants and so she orders hers right away and then goes on to order mine, telling the waiter "...and the lady will have the blackened tilapia." I smile and zone out with my wine, sneaking sidelong glances at my fellow luncheoneers. It's then that I notice that across the room is Larry David.

Larry had hired me to guest star on Seinfeld years ago and we'd gotten along famously. He was very complimentary about how great my episode called 'The Switch' had turned out. Now he was doing 'Curb your Enthusiasm' and I was dying to get a guest star spot. It was my absolute favorite show. I lean in and whisper to Eva "That's Larry David over there." "Yeah, yeah... I saw the bastard..." she answers, not even looking up. "And he's eating with Mel Brooks!!!" I excitedly observe. "Good for him. I hope he chokes," mutters Eva. "Eva! What did Larry David ever do to you?" She takes a big swig of wine and out it comes.

The New York Times had, business as usual, printed an obituary of some old lady who'd passed on, but whoever was in charge of the column that day had apparently forgotten to check the deceased's obit for any typos or misspellings. Instead of describing the dear old thing as so-and-so's "beloved aunt", it read "beloved cunt." All hell broke loose. All the mucky-mucks at the Times, including Eva, were sworn never to speak of it. But one night at a Hollywood cocktail party, a tipsy Eva ran into Larry David. "What's the most outrageous thing that's ever happened at the Times?" he asked. "If you promise never to use this in any way... I'll tell you." Says Eva trustingly. "I promise," agrees Larry David, solemnly raising his hand. And so Eva tells him the story of "Beloved Cunt." Cut to Eva, in bed months later, watching "Curb Your Enthusiasm". Well, what do you know? Larry is in charge of writing somebody's aunt's obituary and mistakenly submits "beloved cunt" to the paper who unwittingly publishes it. Sound familiar?

Well Eva, the only New York Times executive stationed in L.A., was naturally suspected of being the leak; and barely escaped being sacked. "So that lying motherfucker can kiss my ass!" is how she fitfully finishes up. "Well," I say cheerily, "let's not let that ruin our lunch." I pour the rest of the wine and she orders another bottle. We eventually eat, drunkenly chattering on about this and that, and when our bill comes, Eva promptly pays it and gets up to use the lady's room.

As soon as she's gone, not wanting to waste this opportunity, I smile and wave to Larry across the room. He smiles and waves back, really big. He remembers me. He stands up and waves me over. Oh, my god. He's going to introduce me to Mel Brooks, one of my idols. And even better, ask me to guest star on 'Curb your Enthusiasm'. Yes!!! I spring out of my chair to go over but suddenly feel somebody behind me grab the arm of my blazer and push me out of the way. It's Eva. "YOU!" she screams across the restaurant in Larry David's direction. "YOU NO GOOD LYING SACK OF SHIT!!!" Larry's smile disappears and is replaced by a look of sheer terror. "I JUST TOLD MY FRIEND HERE WHAT A FORK-TONGUED FUCKER YOU ARE!" I want, of course to tell Larry David that when she says 'friend', it's just an expression and that I would say 'passing acquaintance' at best. But it's too late... an ashen Larry David has already hurriedly thrown scads of money onto his table and he is literally running out of the restaurant. "YEAH! YOU BETTER RUN, YOU CHICKEN SHIT!" Eva screams after him.

I have a strong feeling the only place I'm ever going to see Larry David again is on my television set. Steaming, I shoot daggers at Eva. "What?!" she asks, shrugging nonplussed. I end our lunch with "Let me just say for the record; if the words 'beloved cunt' ever appear in your obituary, it will <u>not</u> be a typo."

The stomach cramps, which ensue on the way home from that career-killer of a lunch, are nothing compared to the burning sensation traveling up my esophagus. So this is how people get acid reflux. That's it. I'm better off at home with a bowl of cold cereal than with a giant mound of Beluga caviar at one of these Hollywood showbiz freebies. The good news is that since giving up H.B.L (Hollywood Business Lunches, for the new arrivals to Tinsel Town), my upside down gut has righted itself. All my digestive woes are gone. I'm a new man. Except maybe to my relatives. I recently overheard my cousin, Ronald, at a family reunion, say to a much younger cousin whom I'd never met "No shit. He was on SNL in the late eighties." "He was?" asked the young man, incredulous. "Yeah" continued Ronald, "he's your cousin, he's Aunt Lenore's son, Terry." The boy's face, still blank, suddenly brightens. "The one with the nervous bowels?"

"Bingo" says Ronald.

THE CURSE

My know-it-all stepbrother, Russell, seven years my senior, has decided he can fix the electric broom he just broke before our mother gets home. Sitting in his underwear with the machine on his lap, he futzes with a screwdriver, poking here and there and cursing.

"Are you sure you should be fooling with that?" I ask suspiciously. "It says right here in the instructions..."

"Shut up!" He snaps. "And mind your own business! I know what I'm doing."

Apparently he does because one of his lucky pokes turns out to be spot on, and the electric broom starts right up–taking his underwear and his balls with it.

"Aaaaaagh!" An intense cry of agony issues forth from my startled brother. I pull the plug out of the socket as fast as I can and force myself to look. There in front of me sits my brother with an electric broom attached to his now twisted undies, its long shiny aluminum handle sticking straight up in the air like a five-foot metal penis.

"Do something!" My brother screams.

"Dear God, I begin my earnest prayer, help this big dummy." At the time, I was going through a very religious period, my confirmation only a year away, and thought the Lord knew best in any crisis, but apparently my brother preferred a more worldly solution.

"Call 911, you little shit!" He rudely shouted at the top of his lungs. "Alright, alright, calm down!" I yell back completely un-calm myself. I start rehearsing in my mind how best to convey a sense of urgency without having to tell a nice lady police operator the sordid details of what has been sucked up where. Still, I don't want her brushing my call off as some sort of childish prank.

I dial and as soon as I hear a voice, I blurt out hysterically, "Life and death...an electric broom...Hurry! For God's sake, hurry!" Then I add calmly, "444 Broadway, Massapequa Park." Right on cue, my brother, who has tried to move, screams once more, in anguish, "Aaaaaagh!" I gingerly replace the receiver. That ought to get every ambulance in Nassau County speeding over here. And sure enough, it does. You'd have thought a 747 had crashed and taken out our entire block. Paramedics and firemen and police spill out of trucks, ambulances and squad cars, and pour into our house. Where on earth is our mother?

Oh, that's right...Lenore had told us that morning she was going to Copiague to visit Aunt May and her gallstones, which had tickled me at the time since it sounded like a bad musical act you'd book to perform in a nursing home: "Ladies and gentlemen, put your hands together and give a warm Sun City welcome to Aunt May and her Gallstones."

Meanwhile, back at Sweeney headquarters, Lenore's oldest son is being loaded onto a stretcher with her Hoover Electro-Lux Broom still firmly attached to his testicles. Unfortunately, neither the male paramedics nor the firemen are capable of the delicate operation of slowly detangling my brother's scrotum from the complex and very efficient set of brushes that the good people at Hoover bragged put the "lux in Electrolux." I swear I heard a few mumbled off-color remarks and a barely suppressed giggle or two from these alleged

EMT professionals. However that is nothing compared to the laughter and applause as my brother is wheeled out on a gurney. It was as though the whole block thought they were "extras" in a special episode of "America's Stupidest Repairmen." Gossipy housewives in dusters and curlers whispered conspiratorially to one another while other neighbors just scratched their heads perplexed.

"He accidentally vacuumed his balls," I try explaining. "It could happen to anyone," I add, faux matter-of-factly. They are definitely not convinced. I can see the headlines in tomorrow's Newsday, "Teen Goes Nuts with Hoover!"

My mother is gonna kill us both. Him for being such a jackass for fixing that contraption in his underwear and me for calling 911 and dragging the Sweeneys' good name through the mud. Although why she thought we had a good name in the neighborhood in the first place was beyond me. Hadn't she challenged Mrs. Thompson around the corner to come out and fight in the street after Mrs. Thompson (quite accurately) called my brother a "trouble-making little bastard"? Isn't she the one who told the cop who lived next-door not to block our driveway with his patrol car again "if he knew what was good for him?" Or maybe it was simply the time that, banging on a pane of glass in an upstairs window, screaming at some neighborhood kids to get off her newly seeded lawn, she broke the window and shards of glass came raining down onto our front steps. Her cry of "Now you've done it, you little sons of bitches!" was enough to make her "persona non grata" among many of their highly offended mothers. Good God. What is she going to make of this circus-come-to-town freak show starring her family? I don't have to wait long to find out. Through the crowd, Lenore comes charging, her pocketbook dangling wildly from the crook of her arm. There my brother lay in front of her in his full tragicomic glory.

The paramedics have tried to cover his mechanical erection with a sheet, which has only made it worse by creating a sadly comical white pup tent over his privates.

The fire chief explains the situation to my mother and while he does so, Lenore half-listens and at the same time, slowly turns her head to survey the onlookers. Each one of them gets their own personal Sicilian death stare as if to say: "I will remember your face always and you will pay for feasting your eyes on my family's shame." Talk about dispersing a crowd. She grabs my sweaty little hand and drags me with her. We are to follow the ambulance in our car.

Once inside our soundproof 50's tank of a Chevy, she makes me recount every detail leading up to this disgrace. I'm dreading her response. To my utter surprise, she calmly informs me, "It's not your fault," then adds, "It's the Giacalone Curse."

"What curse?" I ask in amazement. "No one ever told me about any Giacalone Curse."

"Well, that's because you're not a Giacalone...and neither am I, but your brother is. That was my first husband's last name, remember?"

"Yeah, but I don't believe there's a cur–"

Cutting me off, Lenore launches into a harrowing tale of Sicilian hocus-pocus.

"Remember when Aunt Anna Giacalone decided to save money and dye her own hair? She never read the fine print on the instructions that said to test it on a few strands to see if you're allergic..."

"Well, nobody does," I try to interrupt but my mother is now far away gazing into an imaginary crystal ball filled with hindsight.

"Well, she should have! That black dye #39 from Clairol made her head swell so big she looked like a deep-sea diver that just crawled out of the Black Sea. Luckily the ambulance got there in time. When they wheeled her out, her own daughter Carol asked somebody, 'What is that thing?' and they said "Honey, that thing's your mother!"

Of course, Carol, being a Giacalone, fainted and cracked open her skull and then she had to go to the hospital two minutes later."

"But that could happen to anybody," I protested.

"But it didn't. It happened to a Giacalone. The worst part was her color came out great. It's never looked that good since," she adds, shaking her head sadly.

"Well, that really doesn't mean there's a curse."

"My first husband? Dead from a brain tumor! A Giacalone!"

"Actually, that's just a medical thing. Lots of people in the world get 'em."

"No!" Says Lenore vehemently. "Lots of people catch colds. Giacalone's catch brain tumors!"

"They're not catching," I volunteer.

"Oh, are you a doctor? What do you know?"

I hold my tongue and sit in silence, thinking, Well, I may be eleven years old, but I do know you don't "catch" brain tumors, even if you drink out of some brain-tumored guy's glass. Jesus! I look over at my mother who is back to shaking her head sadly. I suddenly feel sorry for her. It can't be easy to carry around that much misinformation in one brain.

"And now...your brother. It always comes in threes, doesn't it?" More superstitious mumbo jumbo. But I decide not to waste my time trying to disprove any more of her Sicilian old wives' tales. After all, just yesterday, after pulling a roast out of the oven, she called out, "My ears are burning! Who the hell is talking about me behind my back?" Lady, your head was just in a 450-degree oven! See what I mean? Why bother?

Somberly, my mother turns to me at the next stoplight, "Your brother may never have children after this. You know what that means?"

I take a wild guess, "Uh, the Giacalone curse dies with him, and the world rejoices?"

Ignoring me, she marches grimly ahead. "It means you will have to produce my grandchildren."

Me?! Produce her grandchildren? Suddenly I feel like a prize poodle about to be shipped off to a puppy mill to churn out litter after litter for this crazy woman till my privates wear out. "Mother, me?" I finally ask aloud when the momentary shock wears off.

"Yes, you! You're my only shot now!"

Uh, oh...I think...well, then you better shoot yourself. Perhaps you haven't noticed, dear woman, that I have taken off all my macho Zorro doll's clothes except for his black cape and mask and now have him riding bareback on his black plastic stallion. And I also would venture a guess that you failed to take note of the fact that your pink shoebox at the bottom of your closet (the one with your black suede high heels), is never quite in the same spot where you left it. Maybe because *somebody* has been pretending to walk sexily in them into a make-believe waterfront bar, asking a hunky stranger, "Buy a girl a drink, sailor?" I have a feeling that the average eleven-year-old boy, who will one day marry and produce an heir or two, is more likely to be fantasizing about a grand slam with bases loaded (his Little League team carrying him out triumphantly on their shoulders.) Oh no, my fantasies were way too B-movie bad girl to make me a very good candidate for fatherhood.

"Well, we're here," my mother announces as we pull into the hospital parking lot. For the first time in my life, I start praying for my rotten older brother, the one who couldn't wait to tell me that

Santa Claus was a big fatso of a lie and threw the Easter Bunny under the bus while he was at it. Just for kicks he also added that to still believe in all that made-up holiday fakery at the ripe old age of ten just showed what a gullible sap I was and that all the kids on the block were laughing behind my back. This is the person on whom I must now reluctantly ask God to show his mercy. "Save his testicles, dear lord...oh, and sorry I had to use the word 'testicles' in a prayer." Yuck.

"What are you mumbling?" My mother asks as we approach the Emergency Room entrance.

"I'm praying for Russell, mother."

"Oh," she says, slightly taken aback. "Well, while you're at it, pray these morons don't destroy my electric broom while they're removing it from your brother, but if they do, that it's still under warranty."

"I'll throw that in," I fakely reassure her, thinking to myself that God Almighty who rules over this entire planet and all of its creatures who suffer wars, famines and plagues does not have the time to worry about the fine print on the warranty of your ball-sucking electric broom!

Once inside, I resume my mumbled prayers for my no-good brother.

"Let his pecker be perfect. Let his gonads glow with good health so that he (not me!) may be fruitful and multiply." And on I persist, eyes closed, to get myself through the anguish of waiting. When I open my eyes, I see the sad droopy basset hound face of a doctor heading our way. Oh hell. I can already hear him saying, "I'm sorry, Mrs. Sweeney, but your son, Russell, is now a eunuch, incapable of ever reproducing" Then eyeing me and adding, "Thankfully, you have another son." But instead, he grabs my mother's hand and smiles, "He's going to be fine. It all got twisted up in there, but no real damage. He'll probably be sore for ten days or so I'd say."

I burst into tears.

"Well," says the doctor, "he sure is lucky to have a younger brother who cares that much."

Mother cheerfully chimes right back, "Yes, he certainly is."

Chinese Checkers
and Stolen Meat

Growing up, the mothers on television seemed so wise and comforting. They always knew just the right thing to say. Lenore... not so much. Once in a toy store, when I asked her to buy me an apparently pricey red wagon with polished pine slats on each side, instead of a warm tender maternal apology like... "Mommy can't afford that right now, honey. We'll have to save our pennies." She'd whirled around and snapped, "Whaddaya' think I got a money tree in the backyard that shits twenty-dollar bills?" I couldn't imagine June Cleaver pulling the Beav aside to tell him (like my mother had me)..." See that mechanic over there working on mommy's car? He doesn't know his ass from a hole in the ground. "Or pointing at a salesgirl, "The day she got that job, she stepped in shit." Implying, of course, how easy it was to get the job in the first place and how lucky the dope was to keep it; since according to my mother, "She's got shit for brains."

No, Lenore was definitely a graduate of the Sicilian-Tough-Talkin'-Hair-Pullin'-Take-No-Prisoners School of Life. My aunts would tell me stories of her challenging her prize-fighter brother, my Uncle Paulie, to duke it out whenever he pissed her off. She started wearing lipstick down to the breakfast table when she turned sixteen, and her father would slap her across the face and demand she wash it off. She refused and the very next day, would come down again wearing lipstick and get slapped. This went on for weeks according to my aunt until one day he finally just gave up. My Aunt Jean once told me, "Your mother's so tough, sweetie, that when anybody in the family had a problem with somebody, we didn't send the men...we sent your mother to deal with them!" Later in life, when I was being picked on or facing some scary seemingly insurmountable odds, I was to call on her defiant Sicilian example to pull me through. In some ways she was my 'she-ro'... sort of a Xena Warrior Princess. Unfortunately to tell the truth though, other days she was more like *Xenophobia* Warrior Princess. I was forever running around the house manically closing windows so that innocent passersby wouldn't by chance hear their nationality or religion rudely thrown under the bus. Many of the children in the neighborhood weren't allowed to come over and play...Gee, I wonder why?

When the house across the street went up for sale, I prayed new people with kids my age, who didn't know any better than to buy a house across the street from the Sweeneys, would move in. Finally I'd have some friends to play with, at least till they'd crossed paths with you-know-you. One day, a yellow moving truck showed up out of nowhere and five matching yellow people with almond-shaped eyes came trooping out. I couldn't have been happier...the first Asian family on the block! As I jumped up and down in celebration on my bed upstairs; downstairs I could hear my mother call out melodramatically to the heavens, "WHY ME GOD?! WHYYYYYYYYYYY?!"

It turned out my new neighbors were a lovely multi-generational family with the last name of Checkers. I called them my Chinese

Checkers and I adored them and was fascinated by all the strange, exotic smells coming from the big steaming pots in their kitchen. Their ancient-looking grandmother slaved over those pots for hours on end, barefoot and dressed in some sort of government-issued flour sack with scarlet red Chinese letters up one side. I never asked anyone in the Checkers family what the English translation for them was in case it was "shoplifter," or "writer of bad checks." Being gay, I just assumed that wearing that unflattering raggedy sack had to be some sort of Chinese court-ordered punishment.

My mother did not approve of all the time I was spending over there and warned me over and over to ABSOLUTELY NEVER eat anything offered to me, hinting (none too subtly) that those pots contained the unspeakable.

"Another sign just went up around the corner about a missing cat."

"And?" I asked, perplexed.

"That's the second one this month," she nodded knowingly, like she was the Sicilian Miss Marple. "Maybe those poor people should ask the Checkers if they've seen it."

"I can't believe you're seriously trying to tell me it's boiling away in one of those pots."

"Swear in front of Almighty God," she intones dramatically, "that you're not eating anything over there."

"I swear," I answer unconvincingly.

"If you come down with feline leukemia, don't expect me to go to your funeral!"

One day I innocently brought home a bag of salted watermelon seeds that Grandma Checkers had made. She had rinsed and roasted them in the oven and salted them. It didn't seem there was any harm in breaking my mother's cardinal rule of never eating anything the Chinese Checkers offered. They were only watermelon seeds for

God's sake. They were so good I even accepted their offer to take a bag to go. Once home, I hid the bag in a kitchen cabinet and went upstairs to do some homework. When I came back down, there's my mother, perusing the Reader's Digest and mindlessly munching on the Checkers' watermelon seeds.

"These are delicious," she chirps, "but I don't remember buying these sunflower seeds."

"You didn't. They're roasted watermelon seeds," I blurt out, then add stupidly, "Grandma Checkers made 'em."

Lenore raised herself up from the kitchen table eyeing the bag as though she can just now clearly see a label that reads, "Warning.... Poison...If accidentally ingested, call 911."

"YOU MEAN TO TELL ME THAT I'M EATING WATERMELON SEEDS THAT SOME OLD CHINK SPIT *OUT OF HER MOUTH*?!!!!"

"Well, sorta," I say trying to sound nonchalant, like it's no big deal, but it was way too late for that ploy. She pulled at her hair like a mad-woman, then bit her hand while growling like an animal–a traditional Sicilian sign of extreme displeasure, which precedes the demise of the person who brought it on. I took off up the stairs and locked myself in the bathroom thinking if by some remote chance I was adopted, now would be a good time for my real parents to come and get me.

Somehow I survived Watermelon-gate and doubled my efforts to open my mother's xenophobic mind to Asian culture. Extra credit reports I did that school year were filled with glowing reports of the many contributions of the Chinese civilization. They had titles like, "Imagine a World Without Rice!" And, "Those Chinese...Can They Build Great Walls or What?!" Except for acknowledging the "A's" on their covers, these, of course, went unread by the very person I was hoping to sway.

Still, the following summer, I noticed she had quietly stopped going on and on about the "yellow peril" across the street, and very pleased with myself, I thought...You're making progress bit by bit. You've chipped away at her bigoted hard outer shell. It won't be long now till she cracks...

And crack she did, at the local A&P.

We were in line at the supermarket. My mother was trying in vain to find a copy of the most important news magazine in her life... T.V. Guide. While she marched off crusader-like in search of her Holy T.V. Grail, I took advantage of her abrupt departure to sneak over to the assorted M&M's at another nearby register and while there, seriously mulled over the eternal question, 'plain vs. peanut?' I was completely lost in a tantalizing world of corn syrup and milk chocolate; and that was probably why I didn't notice the impatient Asian woman behind our abandoned shopping cart, move ours out of the way, and push hers in its place. When Lenore suddenly returned, so did World War II.

"Not so fast, Tokyo Rose!" screamed my mother as she grabbed the woman's cart and with a Sicilian war cry, shoved it and sent it careening down the cereal aisle at a hundred miles an hour. This, of course, brought the entire supermarket to an open-mouthed shell-shocked halt. I, myself, was doing my best imitation of a piece of petrified wood.

I'm not with her; my face silently signaled the crowd...I'm with you people.

"Hey, what are you doing standing there with your mouth hanging open. Get over here and help unload our cart."

Oh no! She'd called it *our* cart!!! The jig was up. I raced over and started throwing cans of cream corn onto what seemed like the slowest moving conveyor belt in America.

"C'mon....C'mon," I muttered frantically to the belt.

My mother tapped me on the shoulder and cleared her throat importantly. "I hope you learned something from what you just saw." (For your own good and the safety of others, you should be institutionalized as soon as possible?)

She didn't wait for my answer. Heady with victory, she slipped her thumbs through the loops of her Bermuda shorts and confided to me, "Next time the Japs come, we'll be ready for 'em. Oh yeah!"

***

Terrence Sweeney, my Irish Archie Bunkeresque father, worked as a butcher in the A & P in the Inter-County Shopping Center. The center was situated, as you might have guessed, on a line that intersected two counties. Thus its wildly imaginative name. The supposed highlight of my week every Friday, as my mother grocery shopped, was when I would be sent, against my will, to the Meat Department to watch my father slice up bloody cow carcasses. I think it was one of those take-your kid-to-work-things that was popular back then. All I could think was thank god he didn't work in the County Morgue.

I found it very irritating that my father referred to his four co-workers as the Polack, the German Lady, the Skinny Guinnie, and the Colored Guy. Doesn't anybody have a name? Did he even know their names?

"Yeah," my father would sigh exasperatedly, "Of course they have names," and not ever telling me what those names were; would go right on referring to them as the Polack, the German Lady, the Skinny Guinnie and the Colored Guy.

After several months of observing the exciting career opportunities awaiting me in the Meat Department, my father wrongly decided I was ready to be initiated into its mysteries. He started out quite innocuously. "Sonny boy," (that's what he called me when he was in his Irish philosopher mode), "Don't be a leader, be a follower," (pronounced "follier" no matter how many times I corrected him.) "You see the leaders always get picked off and have to take the blame for all the crap while the 'folliers' blend into the background and get away with murder. That's why your old man turned down 'shop steward.' I'd have had to turn in all the guys who sneak out a couple of steaks down their pants."

Huh? Steaks down their pants? I was momentarily distracted. My young mind trying to picture this perverse scenario. I found myself thinking about the portly no-nonsense German lady with a string of bratwurst stuffed in her lady parts.

Never mind that now. I had to stay focused. My father was just about to get to the shocking Made-for-TV-Lifetime-Movie moment of this seemingly innocent father-son chat.

"You see what I mean? How can I steal meat every day then turn around and turn those bums in?"

"WHAT?!" WAIT A MINUTE!!! Every day of his workweek my father has been coming home with stolen meat down his pants? I have been living off stolen meat?! Me?! And now that he's let me in on his little secret, I'm an accomplice! Being a nice squeaky-clean Catholic kid, I immediately feared for my soul. Maybe I could write the Vatican and ask the Pope for clemency. At least when I die, that might get me bumped up from burning in Hell for all Eternity to picking up trash in an orange jump suit on the side of the Highway to Heaven. What about Lenore? She must be in on it, too. I flashed back to their conversation in the front seat of the car the day before...

> Her: "So whaddya get?"
> Him: "Pork chops."
> Her: "Goddamit! I said lamb chops, not pork chops. Clean out your ears!"
> Him: "Alright, alright. Get off my back. I'll grab ya' some tomorrow."
> Her: "Yeah, well ya' better. I already made the goddamn mint sauce that goes with 'em."

Dear God in heaven...my mother is the 'brains' of the gang. He takes his meat marching orders from her!

Once home, I hastily raced upstairs to my room and reverently took down the painted porcelain 'Christ on the Cross' figurine from my bedroom wall and placed him gently in the top drawer of my bureau. Jesus did not need to see or hear the evil shenanigans of these two unrepentant meat pirates. Before I close the drawer, I gaze down upon Christ's weary face. "Forgive them, Lord...and while you're at it, make me a vegetarian. I beseech thee... Oh, wait a minute, Lord. I just remembered something: could you maybe wait till tomorrow, tonight's my favorite... stolen meatballs and spaghetti."

BULLY FOR ME

I always marvel at people I meet who wax euphoric about middle school. If you're anything like me, you remember for a fact, Junior High School was like prison. You were always happy you had lived to see another day. Certain inmates/classmates picked on you constantly, but you could never tell the warden/principal or they'd make it even worse for you for being a "snitch." The lifers/ bad ass brutes who kept repeating sixth grade were the overgrown homicidal muscle that ran the joint. These were the teenage thugs who kicked my books down the hall and shoved me accidentally on purpose into my locker and wrote 'faggot' on my school books in magic marker when no prison guard/ hall monitor was looking. When cornered by them, you had better be prepared to pony up some sort of bribe/academic ransom as a kind of "life insurance." As in, "I'll write your paper on Socrates, if you promise not to sock-it-to-me next time you see me in the hall." Junior Hell School couldn't end soon enough, as far as I was concerned.

By the time I reached High School, I felt like I'd been transferred to an Honor Farm. My reprieve only marred by two things: my trip to school every morning where I was taunted and threatened by the loud mouth rowdies that sat in the back of the bus and my weekly gym classes. Especially the gym classes where two team captains had to pick their fellow teammates; the boys would fight over me, but not in the good way.

"You take Sweeney! I don't want him!"

"Me?! You take him! I got stuck with him last time"

"Hey, guess what guys, I can **hear** you!"

This sort of shame-filled interaction is probably what pushes some poor kids to jump out of a window. Luckily, my fear of heights was worse than my fear of humiliation at the hands of these numbskulls. I silently wished them all a permanent case of jock itch and prayed for the bell that would blessedly put an end to this dumbed-down Darwinian selection of the fittest. Reluctantly someone would finally add me to their dodgeball/basketball/softball squad where I would spend most of my time in fevered entreaties to God. Things like, "Please don't let that ball find me, Lord," and "Send a plague of locusts to this baseball field so thick they have to call the game... and while you're at it...smite that muscle bound bully of a gym teacher, Mr. Balboa, who keeps blowing his damn whistle at me and screaming in front of everybody... "For Christ's sake, Sweeney! You're pathetic! Keep your eye on the ball!" What ball? Where?!

At the beginning of the summer before my senior year of high school, I was guardedly optimistic. Only one more year of gym and high school horror to go. Although my grades the past year had gone through the roof, I was still vulnerable to bullyesque behavior. It seems D-student dummies do not take your perfect SAT scores into account before deciding whether or not to throw your baloney sandwich out the school bus window. Never mind. Finally it was June. Time off for good behavior. Tragically, that's when my father drops a bombshell that threatens to blow my three-month summer parole from public school right out of the pool water that's been waiting for me all year.

"It's time for you to buckle down and get a summer job, sonny boy." Work?! It's my summer vacation when I give my over-worked bullied nerves a well-deserved rest. Before I can mutter even one word of protest, a tidal wave of my dad's favorite clichés washes over me.

"It's a dog-eat-dog world... "It's nose-to-the-grindstone time"... "If you fall down, you gotta get up fast, or they'll walk all over you and keep on going!" Who? Who is "they"?

I fully expect my over-protective, hovering mother to quickly kibosh this fiendish plot to rob me of my childhood; but instead see her nodding vigorously in agreement with this summer job nonsense. This is the same woman who wouldn't permit her little pampered prince to do any chores around the house. I was not even given the job of cutting the lawn like every other teenage boy because she knew of somebody's sister-in-law's manicurist's son who cut off his toes with a lawn mower. How old was this kid? Two? No matter how hard my father argued to the contrary, my mother refused to allow her son's twinkle toes anywhere near the mower. Where was this madwoman's iron resolve now, when I needed it most? Oh, hell...That's the problem with crazy people. They can be so unpredictable. You can never count on them to give you crazy when you want crazy.

With the same enthusiasm that Christ picked up that giant wooden cross back in Jerusalem, I pick up a Long Island Newsday and peruse the classifieds. I find a 'Help-Wanted' ad for a cashier at the Mays Department store in Massapequa, a short commute from my house. I got pretty good grades in math, so I think...hey...I can do that. I call and somebody on the other end gives me a time to come the next day and interview with the head of personnel, Mrs. Buffalino.

When they said 'head' they weren't kidding. Already cursed by a head that was much too large for her body, Mrs. Buffalino had unfortunately chosen to emphasize it with a huge sprayed mountain of grey hair. Both of which combined to give her the freakish appearance of a Thanksgiving Parade float. To make matters worse, her silver cat-eye glasses somehow strangely magnified her black-brown eyes giving her the otherworldly look of an alien space creature whose saucer, headed for Roswell, had malfunctioned and crashed to earth here in Massapequa.

This may be my first encounter with an extraterrestrial, I think somewhat excitedly. She stares down sourly at my puny job application where I had filled in the blanks that had asked for the names of former employers with useless fluffy after-school activities like the "chess club" and "chorus" and clears her throat. I am sure she is stalling for time while the outer space gibberish in her alien brain is being translated into a language spoken on our planet.

"I run a tight ship," she warns me ominously. (As in spaceship?)

"Don't think I won't know if you goof off. You'll find I have eyes in the back of my head."

Please, God, don't let her turn her head 180 degrees and show me a duplicate set of cat-eyes peering out of the back of her skull or I will surely shit myself.

"Mays isn't just another department store," she self-importantly confides to me.

No, I think to myself, it's where you operate your secret headquarters and plot your future invasion of an unsuspecting Earth.

Just then the "bong...bong...bong..." of May's P.A. System momentarily interrupts our interview. Mrs. Buffalino freezes as though an announcement from the Mother Ship is forthcoming. Instead it's just a hopped-up reminder to folks in the store that

Mays has a "limited-time-only" sale going on right this minute that requires them to take immediate action in order to jump on a once-in-a-lifetime opportunity... "Shoppers...in our Stationery Department...staplers...formerly 3.99...for the next half hour...3.49... while supplies last." I gleefully imagine utter pandemonium on every floor as crazed desperate housewives throughout Mays drop what they're doing and run willy-nilly to the stationary department where they punch and elbow each other in the face to get the last stapler.

"What's so funny?!" Mrs. Battle-ax Galactica demands to know. Oh shit. They can read minds on her planet. I immediately make mine go blank. "Uh...nothing," I stammer back innocently.

"Are you <u>sure</u> you're Mays material?" she asks warily, narrowing her eyes, acting as if she's seconds away from pressing a secret button on her desk that will drop me and my chair through a trap door in the floor. She leans forward studying me intently.

"Hey lady." I wanna yell, "I'm interviewing for a lowly job as a cashier at your mediocre department store, not Chief of Staff at the Mayo Clinic. So back off, Space-bitch!" But remembering my folks waiting anxiously at home, instead decide to improvise something. What the Buffalo lady doesn't know is that on my job application I'd left out "Drama Club." The curtain goes up, and I'm on.

"Mrs. Buffalino, I have been in awe of Mays since I was a child. It's always been a dream of mine to one day be a part of this department store giant. I'm just hoping you'll find it in your heart to make that dream come true." The envelope, please...and the Best Actor in a Department Store Interview is...Wait a minute. She's not exactly reaching for a Kleenex to wipe away the tears. Did I lay it on *too* thick?! No. She gives me a slight nod and the hint of a smile. That answer was apparently music to her ears. If she has ears. I don't see any. God only knows what she really looks like out of her earth-drag.

"I will approve your application with a two-week probation period. During which time, I may terminate you for any infraction whatsoever." I don't like the way she says, "terminate", but I agree to her terms knowing my overeager parents are hoping and praying for me to come back...a May's employee. The apparent equivalent in their minds to bringing home Olympic Gold.

I slump out of May's, depressed and slightly in disbelief that I am holding an actual employee name tag. Even worse, is when the elderly security guard says, "See you tomorrow, kid!" And tomorrow, and tomorrow after that, old man. It's official. A florescent-bulbed summer stretches painfully before me. On the way back home, I'm feeling very sorry for myself, but as predicted the Sweeney household rejoices at the news that their prodigal son was hired. Ding Dong! Ding-dong! You can almost hear church bells ringing throughout the land. The fact that I've been sold into wage slavery and will no longer have time to enjoy what's left of my childhood splashing around in neighbors' pools without a care in the world or happily riding my bicycle through sun-dappled woods does not seem to trouble them in the least. I'm only surprised they haven't thrown my stuffed animals and my Barbies onto a bonfire in the back yard. It's obvious these two can hardly wait for my entry into the grim joyless 9 to 5 adult world of working stiffs.

Immediately, both of them spill over with their version of helpful professional advice. My father is the first to speak from his years of experience: "Don't get on anybody's shit list!" Not exactly Warren Buffet but that's all he's got. While my mother opts for tips on work place hygiene like... "Don't share a locker with a stranger. Who knows what diseases they're carrying? They could easily open your locker and happen to cough into it; next thing you know–you've got T.B.!" It suddenly dawns on me that being at work all day, away from my childhood home, could be a blessing in disguise.

My first day of work at Mays, I show up dressed neatly, hair nicely combed and with a huge chip on my shoulder. Really? Pushing buttons on a cash register? Day in and day out? Really? I hate it already. But up the escalator I go to the main office, where I will be assigned that day's department. I wait with the other cashiers and one by one, they call out our names and what department we're headed to. "Better Dresses," I silently telegraph the ladies in charge..."Better Dresses." That's the department filled with designer gowns, glitzy cocktail dresses, snazzy shoes and other fabulousities dear to my young gay heart. "Better Dresses," I command them telepathically. "Make it mine."

"Terry?" one of them calls out.

"Yes?" I jump forward excitedly.

"The Garden Center"...What the hell?

"Colleen?" they call out right after me, "Better Dresses."

I hear murmurs of congratulations like the little witch has won a new Cadillac in the company raffle.

Actually, she's perfectly nice, but damn it, even though I've only been in the store five minutes, it should be obvious to anyone with eyes, I belong in "Better Dresses." Colleen's sweet. She can see the covetous longing with which I'm eyeing her cash register key. She squeezes my shoulder and whispers, "The guy who works in the garden department is a big, muscle-bound hunk, just so you know."

"Thanks," I wink and smile back. Suddenly, I like this girl. She's definitely my new May's BFF.

Off I head outside to the Garden Center to meet this bronzed Adonis who no doubt is wondering where his lovely young cashier is.

Coming! Actually, my adolescent imagination is already out there. I picture him wrestling with big bags of cow manure in the hot sun, sweat running down from his brow. He raises up his T-shirt to wipe his manly chiseled face revealing God-like six-pack abs that deserve to be worshipped. Can't this damn escalator go any faster?! I tap the rubber handrail impatiently and weave around early-bird shoppers who just stand there staring zombie-like at each floor, before getting on the next set of descending mechanical stairs in slow motion.

Finally, I'm on the main floor. I start to pick up my pace when I am accosted by a woman who is waving a pair of tangerine-orange culottes in my face..."Are these on sale?" She demands to know.

"Probably, Madam." I know the term "madam" is over the top and way too Harrods of London for this schlemiel of a store, but I can't help myself. I just love saying it. "Culottes are last year," I advise her. "They've put them on clearance because they never want to see them again and neither do I...white linen slacks, 3rd floor... now there's a timeless flattering look." Without missing a beat, she tosses the culottes back onto to a messy discount bin and, thanking me, steps onto the Up Escalator. I sigh wistfully. Oh, what I could have done in Better Dresses. Never mind that now... outside there's a savage brute pacing like a caged animal. Mustn't keep him waiting.

I'm out the front door headed for May's tropical paradise. Well now...the word "paradise" may be a bit of an exaggeration. It is surrounded by a ten-foot hideous metal cyclone fence topped with razor-sharp coils of barbed wire. On one side of the large entrance gates, that have been rolled open for customers to enter, is an eight-foot multi-tiered clearance rack also on wheels where plants which are decayed and dying can be purchased for a pittance. Good

God! Stick that rolling plant casket in the back of the garden center. NOT OUT FRONT! This is a nursery not a plant cemetery. No wonder I was sent here first. Like a gay superhero I vow to combat this clearance rack eyesore as soon as I've sorted out my cash drawer.

I head straight for the picturesque primitive Tiki tacky garden shed that houses the cash register, office supplies and other official nonsense. I keep one eye on my money as I count it out and set up for the day, and the other on the jungle of plants outside my window. No sign of Tarzan yet. I loosen my tie. That should get the subtle message across that I'm up for anything. Deciding that may be too subtle, I take off my tie completely and open a button. That's better. I hear someone cursing and rummaging around way back at the other end of the nursery where they keep the garden tools. I close my drawer and peek around the door. Sure enough, I spy two big muscled arms holding up a giant assortment of rakes that unfortunately block his face. Unable to hold on to them all, he keeps losing one and then tripping over it. Obviously, he's not too bright, but who cares? Look at those biceps. I can talk Shakespeare with them. Besides he only has to know the answer to one question: Can he bench press 145 pounds? Cuz that's what I weigh. When he drops another rake, my jaw drops with it. I know that face. It's my gym teacher, Mr. Balboa! He must be summer-jobbing it till school starts back in September.

"SWEENEY! DON'T JUST STAND THERE, HELP ME!!!" he barks irately.

Help you? I think to myself. When did you ever help me? When I was mocked and ridiculed right in front of you, time and time again; what did you do?... Nothing. I'm happy to return the favor.

"I'm not allowed to leave the register," I calmly and officially inform him. "And may I suggest making **two** trips?" the words 'you moron' implied in my condescending and queenly tone of voice. I abruptly turn on my heels and head back into my cashier's shed as though it were the royal palace.

"Hey, get back here!" I hear behind me.

"Sorry, I don't work for you!" I toss back high-handedly.

"Just wait till I put these away," he fumes.

Oh, bloody hell. I must have been crazy to taunt him. Now I've got a raging bully on my hands and I'm out here all alone. This would never happen in Better Dresses. Thanks, Coleen. Maybe you can do the eulogy at my memorial service to make it up to me. I know I'm tired of being picked on, but did I really have to choose here and now to make a stand? There is more angry rattling of rakes and cursing outside the shed door. I am so screwed. I imagine myself stumbling back into Mays Department Store all bloody with my clothes shredded. "I've been raked!" I blurt out to the ninety-year old security guard before collapsing at his sensible black orthopedic oxfords.

Boom. Boom. Boom The shed door trembles.

"Who is it?" I call out in a fakey singsong voice like I'm in a bad play, way off-Broadway. There's another "boom."

Well, someone famous once said the best defense is a good offense. Now who was that? Not Gandhi, not Churchill...Oh, I know... It was my mother, Lenore. She taught me never to take crap off anyone. God bless her. Time to call on my inner Sicilian. I unlatch the door and stare unblinkingly into his giant red face.

"What's wrong with you!?" he bellows like we're back at High School and he's just yanked me out of some losing game that's my fault.

"You! You're what's wrong with me," I answer calmly.

"What?" He asks momentarily puzzled.

"You have never treated me with one ounce of respect. For the past three years of school, you have blown whistles at me, screamed at me and embarrassed me and even worse, let the other boys in gym class feel they had permission to do the same. You call yourself a teacher? What exactly are you teaching? Hate? Prejudice? That it's all right to persecute people because they're different?"

"Well..." he mumbles... "I didn't think..."

"No," I interrupt. "You didn't think...and you didn't care. I hope you're proud of the rotten example you set." There is an awkward silence. Mr. Balboa looks down at the ground, deep in thought.

"Let me guess, you're trying to decide whether to break my leg or my arm? Or just beat me with a garden hose 'cause it won't leave any marks?" When he looks up, he tries to smile, but for the first time, I see a sad look of defeat on his gung-ho super-jock face.

"I'm a jerk, Sweeney."

"I think that was the point I was trying to make," I bravely mumble.

"I'm sorry." He puts out his giant paw for me to shake.

Can this be happening? Have I really slain my first Goliath?

I take Mr. Balboa's hand and shake it, feeling as though a weight's been lifted off my chest and a strange new inner freedom is lifting me up. Is this what the caterpillar that once crawled feels when it becomes the butterfly?

When I get home, of course, Lenore is right there at the front door.

"So?" she asks impatiently. I start to tell her about how I vanquished my first bully in the Garden Center behind Mays, of all places. But the minute she hears the words..."garden center" she's off and running.

"Garden Center? Outside? Christ Almighty! Goddamn that Mays! Go right upstairs this minute and get in that shower!" she yells as she pushes me toward the staircase... "And check for ticks!" I exasperatedly obey. It's okay. It's not important I tell her. What's really important is what happened today changed me ... and maybe even Mr. Balboa, forever.

CREPES OF WRATH

At the end of my Senior Year at fancy pants Middlebury College, all anyone could talk about was their 'big plans for the future'. Things like bumming around Europe for a year...A cross-country road trip in their sporty new car (a graduation present from Mummy) or the one I heard a thousand times... a cushy job with 'Daddy's firm'. "What's your big plan, Sweeney?" "I'm gonna stand on a busy corner' with a 'Will Work for Wine' sign and maybe wash peoples' wind shields," I'd tell my richy rich friends,. They thought that was hysterically funny. "No really, they'd say, "tell us!" I just did but I sensed they wanted a more impressive big plan.... "Well, I don't like to brag but a big-shot business contact of my family's is after me. He's pretty desperate to have me join his company." I answered with fake swagger. Who exactly was my big shot connection?

My Uncle Charlie, my mother's grizzled, scary Mafioso brother who ran a shady restaurant supply business. I could just see myself spending my days in some cheap Bronx warehouse, (my college degree scotch-taped to a grungy wall to remind me I once had brains) quietly weeping while sorting red-stained tablecloths...

Me: "Is this spaghetti sauce or blood, Uncle Charlie?"

Him: "What are you a cop?! Mind your own business!"

No. Let's face it. I have no big plan. Then I think for a minute… food service…isn't that what Judy Garland turned to in the "Harvey Girls" when her mail order bride thing went awry, way out West? I'll work in a restaurant till my "Big Plan" comes along. How hard can it be? I'd never waited tables, but I'd had plenty of practice waiting on my mother who would bark orders at me day and night:

> Her: "Find my eyeglasses!"
> Me: "They're on your head for God's sake!"
> Her: "Go to the refrigerator and get me a Fresca!"
> Me: "Are you now paralyzed from the waist down?"
> Her: "Go upstairs and bring me down my slippers!"
> Me: "Do I look like I have four legs and a tail?"

Yes, I definitely had what it takes to be a snooty waiter. And with that insight, off I go to Boston where I find 'The Magic Pan Restaurant and Creperie' and thanks to my liberal art's degree in Spanish; meet and befriend Anna Gomez, its Mexican crepe maker.

The Magic Pan has a great gimmick. In the main dining room, there is this giant, round mosaic-tiled crepe-making machine. On top of it are a dozen upside-down crepe pans that move in a circle over gas flames. The crepist (that sounds creepy, I know, but that's what they call the person who works the machine) dips the bottom of a hot pan in the batter then turns it over and sends it around the bend to be cooked. Eventually, he or she pulls it off the circulating cooker and flips over the pan and adds the newly cooked crepe to a big, fresh, hot pile of other newly made crepes in the center. That's probably a lot more than you would ever want to know in your lifetime. But if you think it's mind-numbing reading about, you can imagine the monotony of sending crepe after crepe after crepe around this never-ending wheel of misfortune.

My pal, Anna, a somber young Mexican girl with dark skin, big brown eyes, and Aztec-Indian features is the poor soul who has been given the task of working the crepe wheel. What had she done to deserve this terrible fate? Had she been Hitler in a past life? Stalin? The Donald? (Wait a minute, that one still walks the Earth. We can rule him out for now.) Anyway, night after night, my stone-faced Mexican maiden friend, dressed awkwardly in a corny brightly colored Austrian dirndl stares into the abyss, robotically making crepe after crepe after friggin' crepe. What, I wondered, is she thinking? If that were me it'd be... Somebody bust me and send me back to Mexico! Call La Migra, I dare you! I have stolen this job from your American children! What are you waiting for?! Report me! ... But not Anna. She calmly carries on without even the slightest display of temperament. Saint Anna...we call her.

The tourists, whenever they come to the restaurant, are absolutely enthralled by the crepe wheel. They act like that crepe-making thing-a-ma-jig is the eighth wonder of the world. Gathering around it, they ooh and ahh and gasp as Anna flips the next crepe onto the crepe pile as though they have just witnessed dead Jesus roll the stone back at Gethsemane and emerge alive once more. A barrage of questions always bombarded the stoic Anna: "What's in the batter?" "How long did it take you to learn to do this?" "Have you ever burnt one?" "Who invented this machine?"

From what I can tell, Anna only knows two phrases in English— at least that's all I'd ever heard her speak—"Sorry de bus late," and "I go home now." Neither of which provide much insight into the pans that "magically" spin before her. Could the restaurant have hired someone who speaks English and is better equipped to deal with the tireless inquiring minds of its customers? Yes, of course. But that would have cost them an extra nickel. God only knows what poor Anna was making. For all I knew, they paid her in shiny beads and tequila.

Since I speak fluent Spanish, I try to coach her on how to deal more assertively with her constant crowd of looky-loos. But she will have none of it. Too bad. They're great ideas like sticking her thumb to her nose and waving her other four fingers in a kiss-my-ass-gringo salute, or grabbing a hot crepe pan and waving it menacingly at the startled tourists, screaming, "Dees is bull sheet! Dere ees no magic! Go back to your homes you stoopid pieces of white bread!"

No, no. She is much too demure for any of that nonsense; but still it secretly tickled her to see me act out my crazy scenarios when no one was looking. You see I am standing not far from her at the host's station. Yes I said the host's station. Although I'd had four years of college and been president of the National Honor Society during my high school tenure, none of that had apparently prepared me to ask the simplest of questions such as "Can I take your order?" Or to carry plates of food or refill water glasses.

"You're not ready," I was told solemnly by a dorky manager with horn-rimmed glasses and whiskey on his breath. No, instead he posts me at the front desk. When someone walks in, I am to be the first happy shiny face to welcome them.

Although not thrilled with the situation at first, I must say, I am good at it right from the start. I adopted a grand manner that made customers think it was my restaurant. I am Le Gaytre'd! I try to make the most of my new role. In those early weeks, I am attentive and courteous, warm and friendly, whatever they want me to be. I am a front of the house happy hooker with a clip on tie and I aim to please. But after a while, making minimum wage while waiters with pockets bulging with cash are parading back and forth in front of me, gets old. And to make matters worse, it has occurred to customers that though Anna "no speakee Eeenglish"; the nice blue-eyed, blond-haired young man nearby does and can probably answer all of their burning questions. Hundreds of them. After a while, it starts to take its toll. To keep from going mad, I make stuff up.

"It's called The Increperator. It's based on a rotating instrument of torture used in the Spanish Inquisition"; "The batter is blessed by the Pope and is then sent on huge tankers to America where it is hosed into giant underground vats in case of nuclear war"; "Where is Anna from, you ask? Haiti...she's part of our Zombie Affirmative Action program. The first of its kind in the States."

Meanwhile, the experienced waiters continued to scoop up their booty left and right while I suffered in silence. Help me, Lord, I fervently prayed. And he did. The next day, one of the waitresses fell down the front steps of her brownstone. Now I'm not saying the Lord pushed her, but He does work in mysterious ways. Feeling a little guilty, I send her flowers and promptly grab her spot on the schedule. I follow a waiter around on my first night; the second night, I am thrown in the deep end...sink or swim. I sink. I break not one sweat but two, running around in circles, "Where's our dinner?!"; "You forgot my soup"; "Could I have hot tea, if it's not too much trouble!"; "This is ice cold!"; "We've been waiting twenty minutes! How come they got their food? We were here first! Where is ours!? And ours?! AND OURS?!!!"

I am a wreck. A far cry from the civilized "Host with the Most" who once coolly had command of the room. So this is why the waiters make all that moola. Well, they can have it. At the end of this shift, I shall inform the management I was born for better things. This has been an interesting experiment. I shall write my Master's Thesis on it and call it, "Let Them Eat Crepe!"- Linking the beheading of Marie Antoinette to rampant low blood sugar among the masses and gluten intolerance. Meanwhile, will this torture ever end? I suddenly remember that at the end of this shift I am entitled to a complimentary shift drink. Oh, thank-you God. Is it time yet? I check my watch. Oh hell... I've only been working for twenty minutes.

Six hours later, I crawl to the bar to get my "free" drink. I scan all the bottles taking forever to decide what it will be. Finally, Rich, the hot straight bartender (with the bushy porn star mustache) can't take it anymore.

"Hey, Sweeney, spit it out!"

"Uh....Dewar's and soda with a twist." I really want a glass of white wine, but Dewar's and soda with a twist is what Rich drinks, and I am trying to show him how much the two of us have in common. He is sooo cute. I smile, thinking the poor guy doesn't have a clue that I've been working on getting him into the sack. He hands me my drink.

"By the way, I'm straight and I plan to stay that way. Give it up."

Okay, obviously I'm not the subtle genius I thought I was. I slink away from the bar thinking this is the perfect ending to my first and last night as a waiter in this 'craperie'.

I pull out my money and morosely count it. What? How much? I made a hundred and fifty dollars in one night?! Suddenly I'm twirling around the empty dining room like Julie Andrews in "The Sound of Music".... "The Hills are alive, with the sound of money!"

Perhaps I was too hard on those dear sweet people, a.k.a. my customers. Perhaps my virgin waiter ears were just a tad oversensitive.

Tomorrow night I will most definitely incorporate more bowing and scraping maybe even a curtsy..."My name is Terry and it is my great honor to be your humblest of food servants."

That night, I walk Anna home to her apartment and we both agree: the magic wheel of pans will have to take care of us both till we each discover "El Grande Plan Por El Futuro..." Oh Anna, I'm gonna be stuck here till God knows when." "Me too..." Anna sadly chimes in. I'm depressed realizing deep down how much she must hate that wheel and never ever has said a word. What good would it do? Suddenly a way out for Saint Anna occurs to me "...How 'bout tomorrow night you pretend to go berserk and write 'Eat shit and Die!' in crepe batter on the mirror behind you?" I bet we could get you some kind of Psychiatric Worker's Comp.

"Oh, Terry," she smiles, shaking her head, "You crazy."

CINDERFELLA

Who doesn't dream of a beautiful glass slipper that will one day come along and fit their foot perfectly and magically transform them from long suffering servant to princess? All I know is here I am now in Manhattan, still a food servant night after night. The only magic in my life is still The Magic Pan, the chain restaurant I transferred to from Boston to New York. But how many hundreds of times can you ask if someone wants whipped cream or sour cream with his strawberry crepe before you lose the will to live? I don't know but I'm close. I need a call to greatness. Instead what I get is a call from my friend, Mr. Jimmy, calling to cancel lunch.

"My agent says they're hiring writers over at Saturday Night Live. I've gotta get my stuff to him this afternoon so he can send it over."

"Hey..." I say out loud, "I wonder if I should write some sample sketches for Saturday Day Night Live?"

"Don't bother, he says, you're too late. The cut off for applying is today!" Click.

"Hello? Hello....Helloooo...."

Well, that's that. Or is it? ...Maybe I can still...?

The evil stepsister that lives in my Cinderfella head is quick to taunt me. "You don't have an agent. You have no connections and no experience. You don't even know how to type! You? Get a job writing for Saturday Night Live?!"

Cue: Villainous mocking laughter.

I sigh. Defeated before I even start. Back to "...whipped cream or sour cream with that strawberry crepe?"

No!

If I'm already a loser, I have nothing to lose. Beat it, sister. I'm gonna give it a shot.

I lock myself in my studio apartment, turn off my phone and turn my coffee maker up to its party-mode max: sixteen cups. I'm gonna need every one. I begin writing sketch after sketch. I'm in the "zone"—and this is before the "zone" has been invented. By eight o'clock that evening, I have a giant pile of what I think is some very funny shit. Or maybe just a pile of shit. I'll soon find out. But first, I must get this stuff typed or they're going to think over at SNL that I'm a total amateur (which I am!). Pages torn out of a spiral notebook? I can see the producer now holding them up in a conference room for the newly hired staff to see. "Ouch" is all she can think to say as waves of snickering and eye rolling fill the room. What am I going to do? I can't turn them in in this state.

I call my friend, Judy. "Please, please please type my sketches," I beg. She's already got plans for the evening. Let me tell you, after sixteen cups of coffee, it's not hard to burst into tears with the slightest provocation. In response to my barrage of uncontrollable sobbing, Judy, desperate to make it stop, quickly adds, "But I can cancel them."

I cease my crying instantly. "I'll be right over," I say and happily gather up the pages. I suddenly realize what a mess they are. Cross-outs here, there and everywhere and extra jokes scribbled helter skelter all over the margins. "Oh sweet Jesus, help me—even though I haven't been to Sunday mass in a while. Keep in mind, J.C., I easily could have become a Buddhist when all my cool vegetarian, yoga-loving hipster friends did. But instead, I stuck by you. Now, for Christ's sake, help Judy decipher my chicken scratch!" In the cab over, all I can hear in my fevered brain is my friend's dire warning…"You're too late…You're too late…You're too late."

The next day I take the subway to midtown, clutching with white knuckles my freshly typed sketch file, like somebody on the train might try and snatch 'em. At this point, even if I dropped 'em on the third rail of the subway tracks, I'd dive in after 'em. Finally, it's my stop, and I get out and head up the stairs to walk the rest of the way to 30 Rock.

I don't remember one step of that walk, but once there, trembling from a sleepless night and even more morning coffee that I probably should have skipped, I step inside 30 Rock's magnificent marble foyer as if in a dream and take in its sights, and smells and sounds. Everybody seems in a hurry. Headed no doubt to V.I.P closed-door board meetings or their plush offices where they will send out memos that will one day revolutionize the way we live. That may sound a tad melodramatic but try not to judge. I have ten gallons of Columbian coffee coursing through my veins.

I sneak over to a nearby newspaper kiosk and pretend to peruse the various publications. But really, I'm eyeing the two black security guards across the way that are standing guard behind a podium with a large NBC logo emblazoned on it. Their stern, no-nonsense demeanor never changes as they check IDs and solemnly examine the day's appointment log to make sure that the person standing before them is legit. Wordlessly they give the nod to official visitor after official visitor without even the trace of a smile.

Oh, hell. This has all been for nothing. They're never going to let me pass. I mean look at me. Red-eyed and rumpled, in clothes I picked up off my bedroom floor. I was in such a rush to get here, I didn't even shave. I catch a glimpse of my reflection in the kiosk's glass partition. Even I'm ready to call a cop and have myself hauled off. Oh, no. I look like I have no business going up to SNL. No business at all. As I stand there, people pass me right and left with their to-go orders from the deli across the way. That's when a light bulb goes off in my head.

Into the deli on the ground floor of the building I go. Minutes later, I'm ordering sandwiches, coleslaw, potato salad, and drinks; as many and as much as I can afford. With arms filled with white bags with napkins and straws sticking out of them and my sheaf of sketches hidden under them, I head for the NBC podium and the "Moment of Truth." Or in my case, the "Moment of the Great Lie."

"Lunch for Saturday Night Live," I blurt out and boldly shove the entire deli mishegas at the largest and meanest looking of the two guards.

"Don't give it to me!" he snaps. "Get in that elevator and do your job!"

"Sorry, Sir," I mumble apologetically. The other brother with him, eyeing me suspiciously, asks, "What happened to Luis?"

Luis?! Luis?! Luis who?! Oh, no. He must be the regular delivery guy.

While my mind reels, my mouth opens, "He won the lottery! Bought himself the biggest house in Puerto Rico."

"I thought he was Mexican," the other guard brusquely interjects.

"Did I say Puerto Rico? I meant Puerto Vallarta" Shut up, already and get going, Terry.

I whiz past them and press the elevator button without so much as a glance back. I tap my foot nervously waiting in my own private hell for the friggin' thing to get there.

"Luis won the damn lottery," one of them gasps in amazement.

"Can you believe that bullshit?" says the other. "I'm gonna get me another twenty bucks worth of Powerball at lunch. Fucking Luis, a millionaire! Man, that shit's crazy."

Yes, crazy shit is exactly what it is. Lord, don't let Luis come strolling up with a pastrami on rye and some bagel chips for some nitwit up at NBC headquarters. The world's slowest elevator finally arrives and I hop on. I'm a nervous wreck. I take deep breaths to try and calm myself.

Keep it together, Terry, you're almost there.

I stop at every floor and peek out. Nothing. Finally the elevator arrives at the floor I've been dreaming about. When I peek out, there at the end of the hallway are two glass doors. Behind them a receptionist sits at a large desk which has Saturday Night Live splashed across its front in neon. My heart quickens and a smile starts to creep across my face; until I notice a small desk where a big burly pockmarked guard sits, with a gun in a holster, no less. He must be there to protect the various celebrities who are coming in to talk about hosting the show. I didn't expect him. No turning back now, here goes. I march directly up to his desk. He's reading some crazy wrestling rag with photos of red-faced guys in chokeholds. Nice.

"Lunch for SNL!" I manage to barely croak out. He just glares at me saying nothing and furrows his Cro-Magnon brow. Could it be that genius here is trying to figure out what S.N.L stands for? I quickly clarify just in case, "Saturday Night Live?" And even point in the direction of the office a mere three feet away. Now we're talking, or at least I am. He wordlessly jerks a giant thumb in the direction of the office. I politely offer a quick and unnecessary, "Thanks!" Like this brute appreciates good manners and will remark on them to my would-be-employers at SNL when they seek his much valued opinion. Now all I have to do is get past the thin-lipped, red-haired young woman on the other side of the glass doors who looks bitchy, busy, and ready to bite someone's head off.

I push open the door and respectfully tiptoe in. Just as I thought, she's having a not-very-nice conversation with some poor slob who's simply asking when can he come today to paint one of the offices.

"Not today...absolutely no painting today. The Executive Producer cannot stand the smell of wet paint and frankly, neither can I. Have I made myself perfectly clear?!" she hisses. What a bitch!!! I want to turn and run but instead manage to mouth the word, "Lunch." She holds up one finger to me with a long, scary red nail on it, in a just-a-minute gesture.

"Well, that's just too bad," she tells that poor painter and hangs up on him. Now it's my turn for the hot seat. Narrowing her eyes at me, she asks almost accusingly, "Lunch?" Lord, me again... please don't let her look around and ask loudly, "Did anyone order lunch?"

I can almost hear the chorus of "No's" and see her pressing a warning bell under her desk, which the bloodthirsty guard in the hallway has been trained like a Rottweiler to react to. With his hand, already on his holster, he would finally have his excuse to shoot to kill at long last. Hey, remember I did say, "Thanks" back there, meathead... doesn't that count for something? Not in his world. I'd probably try to make a run for it but go down in a hail of bullets. My corpse, splattered with German potato salad and turkey with Russian dressing, would end up face down in a lake of diet Pepsi. Hauled off to the city morgue, the building's janitor would be called in to clean up the crime scene. Out of paper towels, he'd use my unread sketches to mop up the bloody mess.

Instead, miraculously, another phone line lights up; then another and another. At her wit's end, the receptionist snaps, "Just go in!" I pass writers' offices and see a few have already been hired. They are unloading book boxes, putting up pictures and fiddling with their new desks. At the door of the corner office, I stop momentarily, then taking a deep breath, I knock and mumble, "Lunch for Saturday Night Live." Not waiting for an answer, I go in and walk right up to the large Executive Producer's desk.

"I didn't order..." she begins saying...I quickly cut her off before I lose my courage.

"Please read my sketches and consider me for a job on your show." I drop the file full of my sketches on her desk and she looks down at it quizzically. Then I gently lay the deli order along side it. "Oh, and lunch is on me..." I smile politely and skedaddle the hell out of there, the way I'd come in. I don't breathe 'til I am once more outside of 30 Rock.

Two weeks pass and not a word. She probably dropped my sketches into the circular file on the floor next to her desk, otherwise known as the wastebasket.

Oh well, I tried.

On my way out the door to The Magic Pan to sadly work another painful shift on the restaurant chain gang, the phone rings. I pick it up and a woman's voice I don't recognize says..."Hello, this is Jean Doumanian. I read your sketches...and they're hysterical. I want you to come in." I feel tears running down my face and try to calm my voice and sound professional.

"Yes...yes, Ma'am."

"And may I ask you something?' She adds.

"Sure," I stammer.

"Where have you been? What do you do?"

"Uh...I'm a waiter."

"Not anymore," she says. "Starting tomorrow...You're a writer."

Turns out somebody up there had a glass slipper in my size, after all.

It's About a Toy Poodle

It is at a lively drinks party that's supposed to be our cheery send off to Lalaland, that our well-meaning New York literary friends choose to warn us about L.A. No, I take that back. "Warn" doesn't seem a strong enough word. The more they drink the more they "terrorize" Lanier and myself with over the top dark tales of Machiavellian duplicity and Julius Caesar knife-in-the-bac k-never-saw-it-coming betrayals that have apparently befallen all the East-Coast-turned-West-Cost scribes they know. One Broadway playwright pal of mine, an avowed Hollywood-hater, predicts ominously: "You'll end up an alcoholic like every other Hollywood writer I know...doing tequila shots at breakfast." No way. Not me. I get up with some difficulty and raise my glass... "Don't worry, people. I have no intention of letting L.A. do a number on me. I'll come back the same New York jaded cynic you know and love." "Here! Here!" They toast back as convinced as I that I've been properly inoculated against the Hollywood birdbrain flu.

Oh yeah? I'm in L.A. a mere two weeks before I find myself riding down Sunset Boulevard in a rented convertible with the top down...oohing and ahhing and pointing wide-eyed at the giant movie billboards like I'm Ellie Mae Clampett. I can't stop thinking how beautiful everything looks. It's the light. No one told me how different the light is out here. But I sure wish they had. We paid $5,000 to have all our New York apartment furniture trucked across the entire United States. But in the blazingly brilliant California sunshine, my cherished flea market antiques I had once thought so English and classy, look like a musty collection of old junk that was hauled out of The Miss Habersham Home for the Aged. No matter where in the mid-century modern L.A. house we rented that we try it, it looks like granny just went to the store to get something to help keep her false teeth from popping out; but she's expected back any minute. Finally, we just stick it all in a storage room and pretend a senile elderly couple that rented the place before us, absentmindedly left it behind.

We buy new stuff, of course, that has a cool late 50's/early 60's California vibe to it. A stainless steel juicer in the kitchen for my now organic veggie juices and bio-dynamically grown fruit smoothies is my latest and most cherished possession. The New York voices in my head, however, are not impressed and have started giving me shit: "You're losing your critical New York Edge...You've gone way too L.A.!" "Nonsense." I shoot back as I sort through my new "hang ten" vintage surfer T-shirts and match one up with a pair of my orange and hot pink Hawaiian surf shorts. "Oh, really?" snipe the voices. "Look at all this crap... Surf? You don't even know how to swim!"

I don't need this today. I'm tired of New York trying to acid rain on my L.A. Parade. I peruse some self-help books I picked up at a trendy metaphysical bookstore out here called "The Bodhi Tree." I need to clear my thoughts now more than ever. Get the positive energy flowing and blow it out my chakras especially since tomorrow, Lanier and I have our first important movie pitch over at Disney. Imagine...Walt Disney...a childhood icon...his very studio...

somebody pinch me. "Want to hear the low down dirty scoop on ol' Walt?" "No!" I bark back at the nasty New York voices. I said, "Somebody pinch me," not "Somebody slap me and throw a bucket of cold water in my face!" To drown out their tragic Greek chorus, I jam on a pair of headphones and turn on my Walkman. (Yes, I know that makes me sound ancient, but that's what there was at the time. So back off before I hit you with my Barbara Stanwyck Big Valley lunch box). Anyway, on my Walkman is playing some "I'm okay...you're okay" tape I just bought that's full of positive affirmations. You know..."See everyone in a bubble of love," that kind of stuff. There we go, I tell myself...that's better. "Release the negativity...surround your world in white light." I know one thing. I'm going to surround that damn meeting tomorrow with white light if it kills me. Uh oh. That sounds a bit overanxious like the old Manhattanite me. I yank off my headphones and closing my eyes try to meditate my inner New Yorker away. As I loudly hum "Om," I catch myself still impatiently tapping one foot. C'mon, inner peace. I don't have all day.

Next morning, we're off bright and early to pitch our film to Disney. Normally, I practice my spiel while Lanier drives but today, the new L.A. me focuses on centering myself and being the positive presence of love. Besides, this movie should be a very simple sell. It's about a toy poodle that's left 100 million dollars when its rich eccentric old lady owner kicks the bucket. Her greedy relatives, all of whom were counting on their share, plot and scheme throughout the movie to do the teeny weeny darling in. It's called, "The Heiress." It's silly g-rated fluff; I know...just your basic fun-for-the-whole-family frolic. But let's face it: It's got Disney written all over it.

We excitedly drive through the Disney studio gates where our names have been left, and park in the lot. It feels a bit surreal to stroll past Dopey Drive and Daffy Duck Boulevard. Some goofy studio employee even rides past us on a bicycle that has a pair of you-know-whose mouse ears on the handlebar. We tra-la-la along till we spot the big shot executive's VIP bungalow where we'll be pitching. I hate to admit it but I silently surround it in extra white light just in case. We quietly slip in the front door that opens onto his waiting room. Smiling politely, we nod to his secretary who looks back at us blankly. "Uh...Sweeney and Laney? We have a ten o'clock appointment?" We still get nothing, except her pinched puss. "Did I get the day wrong?" I inquire, embarrassed. "No," she sighs all pissy, "take a seat." Don't let her throw you off your game, Terry. I hastily conjure up a bubble of love with that bitch's face on it. That's it...stay positive.

In the next room, we suddenly hear shouting. "YOU FUCKING PIECE OF SHIT! IF YOU THINK YOU CAN FUCK ME OVER LIKE THIS AND GET AWAY WITH IT, YOU ARE DEAD FUCKING WRONG!!!"

Oh no, tell me that's not who we're here to see. We look at each other alarmed and then over at the secretary for reassurance. She buries her face in some paperwork. 'I don't hear anything, and you don't either', is her silent message. "LISTEN, SCUMBAG... THAT'S RIGHT...I'M CALLING YOU A SCUMBAG... DON'T YOU HANG...DON'T YOU FUCKING HANG UP ON ME!...MOTHERFUCKER!"

The crash of a receiver hitting its cradle clearly indicates to us that the "scumbag" in question has had enough of this insane verbal abuse and has indeed disobeyed and abruptly ended the call. We get up to leave. "I think we'd better reschedule to some other time when he's..." Cutting me off, she hits the intercom button and announces matter-of-factly, "Your ten o' clock is here." Then nonchalantly to us, adds, "Go right in."

Apparently, she's quite used to these four-letter scream fests, but we are not. "Steady," I tell my jangled nerves..."Steady."... I'm like a jockey trying to coax his spooked thoroughbred into the starting gate. "Light and love"...I inwardly chant. "Buddha, Jesus... Santa...somebody please be with us." We step timidly into his adjoining office.

"Hellooo!" I nervously sing out way too loudly and embarrassingly girly. He doesn't even glance up at us. He's still staring at his phone and maniacally drumming his fingers on his desk. We apprehensively take our seat; sinking gingerly into his two leather office chairs like we're about to have electrodes attached to our balls. More drumming of fingers and no talking. Does he even know we're in the room? Lanier and I look at each other like...Now what? I clear my throat and quietly suggest in a funereal whisper, "If you'd like us to come back another time, we have no problem with that..." Suddenly, his eyes abruptly shift to us. "No....no...No!" He huffs. "Let's hear what you got." I very tentatively begin, "...it's about a toy poodle..."

"Yeah?!" He shoots back gruffly.

Taken aback, I have to collect myself and start again. "It's about a toy poodle that is..." Out of nowhere he angrily blurts out, "Yeah, right! That's what you think!!!" But he's not talking to me. He's staring into some faraway black hole with his lip curled in disgust.

Now normally this is where I would whip out a visual aid. In this case, the cutesy-poo picture of a tiny white poodle I'd cut out of a kid's magazine called 'Woof' that I'd found in my dentist's waiting room. But my hands are shaking too badly to do that and even if I could, he'd probably rip it into a thousand pieces and make me eat it.

"It's called 'The Heiress,'" I say.

"It's a comedy?!" He interrupts with a mixture of hostility and disbelief.

Well, it was definitely a comedy on the drive over, I think to myself; now I'm not so sure. "Yes, it's a comedy...and like I said, it's about a toy poodle..."

"Uh huh, uh huh...it's about a toy poodle," he repeats after me robotically but his rage-filled red eyes are back on his phone. He suddenly jerks the receiver to his ear and hits re-dial. While it's ringing, he barks at us "C'mon keep talking! C'mon! C'mon!" I nervously begin once more, "Well... this toy poodle..." The caller picks up and I freeze. "THAT'S RIGHT. I'M CALLING BACK, ASSHOLE. I JUST WANNA TELL YOU, YOU'RE FUCKING WITH THE WRONG GUY! THE WRONG FUCKING GUY!" By now, I'm guessing whoever's on the other end of this call totally agrees with that statement and wishes to God he'd never met this psycho in the first place, let alone gone into business with this nut. For that matter, he's probably wishing he never heard of Walt Fucking Disney. I know that's what I'm wishing.

When he hangs up, he waves me on impatiently and snaps, "It's a comedy about a toy poodle...got it!...Okay....Okay! Is this thing funny?" he asks making a face like he just drank his own urine sample by accident. "Oh, yes!" Lanier bravely interjects, then peters out unconvincingly mumbling, "It's got lots of laughs." Poor Lanier raises his eyebrows at me to save him and jump in with some hilarious examples. Like the ones we'd come up with all week long that had had us in stitches. I rack my brain for even one. Nothing. All I got is white light. Not that it matters. In the eternity I am taking to come up with even one remotely funny moment; His Craziness has turned his attention back to his phone. He's obviously thinking he let this guy off too easy. Another punch of his re-dial and he's back. But this time, all he gets is the poor man's machine. As soon as he hears the beep, his nostrils flair and the smell of napalm once more fills the air.

"I WILL TEAR OFF YOUR HEAD AND SHIT DOWN THE HOLE! DO YOU HEAR ME?! DO YOU HEAR ME?!! YOU ARE FUCKING FINISHED IN THIS TOWN, YOU FUCKING JERK OFF! FINISHED!"

To get the full effect, you must imagine the word "finished" being screamed at the top of somebody's lungs while white raging spittle foams out of the sides of their mouth. Speaking of finished, Lanier and I jump up to leave.

"Thanks for your time," I automatically politely pipe up. Yeah. Thanks for the 'post-traumatic pitch syndrome' that will probably haunt me the rest of my life. It wouldn't surprise me if every time I come across a toy poodle in the future I throw up and soil myself both at the same time. With his twisted mind a million miles away, this is what we get back from Nutsy, "Yeah...yeah...tell your agent I'll think about it."

Think about what? We never ever told the raving lunatic what the movie actually is, except it's about a toy poodle! I don't care anymore. I am just too happy to get the hell out of that bungalow alive. We don't walk...we run to our car. Still shaking, I glance over at the dashboard clock that reads a mere 10:30 a.m.

"Are there any bars open this early?" I ask Lanier.

"I don't know," he answers. "But I'm gonna find out."

Ten minutes later we're at Joe's Taste of Mexico chugging frozen margaritas and *trying* to get brain freeze. We need to forget.

"Hey, it's our first Hollywood pitch." I say, in a vain attempt to be positive again...."They'll be others." Oh crap, that's right. They'll be others. "Oh waiter, another round! And this time, forget the Margarita mix and the ice; just bring us two shots of tequila.

FIFTY SHADES OF CHEROKEE

The delivery truck pulling up in front of the classic, rustic, built-in-the-Sixties Topanga cabin we just rented can't seem to make up its mind. It brakes; then lurches forward to the bigger house next door; then slowly backs up again. I rush out the front door and wave. The big bruiser of a driver sticks his head out the window and yells "Scuse me, lady - is this 13 Old Canyon Drive?" Lady?!! Okay, so my hair is past my ears and I could maybe use a trim but really! To prove my manhood, I plunge down a couple of octaves to my deepest basso profundo, "Yep... this is it, bro", I answer back; trying to sound more Barry White and less Betty White. "Oh...sorry fella...the sun was in my eyes" lies the delivery man. Sure, sure whatever, I don't care. My new bed and box spring are here. Tonight will be our first night living out in the woods of Topanga Canyon. A full forty minutes away from L.A.; the city I have an ongoing love/hate relationship with.

To me, Hollywood is like a beautiful, bitchy, bipolar frenemy who only calls you when she needs something then forgets you're alive. You know she's crazy, but somehow you forgive her and let her back into your life and guess what?! She totally screws you all over again. That's why I've headed for the hills... the hills of Topanga, that is. Unlike her narcissistic, cold-hearted sister, Topanga is a wild child hippy chick with flowers in her hair who smells of sage and pine needles and patchouli oil who's there for you with a joint and a hug when you need it most.

Topanga, historically, has always been a hide-away for the troubled non-conformists of society: blacklisted writers from the McCarthy era, Vietnam war conscientious objectors, and nudists were among those who once sought refuge in the soft green folds of her perfumed chaparral. She's still to this day home to a tie-dyed patchwork quilt of potheads, rock stars, and back-to-the-land visionaries. Perhaps here, way out in this Woodstock-like Wonderland, even me, Mr. High-Strung with the nervous system of a small white rabbit can learn to chill out and actually experience mellow-hood. I can easily see myself spending my days raising chickens, growing my own biodynamic baby arugula and brewing organic manure tea to pour on my cottage roses. Why right now, Lanier is off buying firewood for the pot-bellied stove in our knotty pine paneled living room. Just saying the words "pot-bellied stove" lowers my blood pressure instantly and who knows, maybe even my cholesterol.

Back to reality… these two muscle-bound brutes are sweating and cursing, trying to squeeze my brand new box spring around a tight corner and through the old-fashioned undersized doorframe. "Are you sure you got the right size bed for this room?!" One of the macho men barks, giving me the hairy eyeball. "Don't worry. I measured. This bedroom is a perfect fit for a queen. You men are just going to have to push harder until it's in!" Somehow that remark coming from me inspires both fear and adrenaline in those two. A couple of manly grunts and a Herculean push later and it miraculously slides in, followed by the mattress.

Two weeks later, Lanier and I have happily settled in and are mixing it up with our fellow Topangans at a large neighborhood party. I chance to meet an attractive salt-and-pepper-haired former Wall Streeter named Grant and his beautiful young wife Rainbow (somebody's hippy parents dropped a lot of acid!). After overhearing me tell some long-haired dude in a Grateful Dead tee shirt, that I'd actually come to Topanga to meditate and that I was looking forward to a good, old-fashioned make-love-not-war rest of the summer; Grant pulls me aside and tells me he has just the thing for me and my man (as he puts it). It seems he and Rainbow are going to a sex seminar this weekend that I might be interested in. Oh, my God. I'm being hit on by a couple of Topanga swingers. Pardon me, but do I look like the type who would be up for a bong and a bang or a bump and a hump or whatever you two pervs got going on?! Before I can give him my indignant brush-off, the very next thing out of Grant's mouth is "Now, I don't want you to think we're a couple of swingers hitting on you. We would never do that." You wouldn't? Never? Why not?! My righteous indignation suddenly changes its tune and 'What-am-I-chopped-liver?' is now playing on my inner jukebox. I try to turn the volume down so I can hear what Grant's saying now, "It's a Native American Weekend Sex Seminar... you'll really be amazed by what you'll learn. The Cherokees totally had a unique take on sex. It'll blow your mind." "Well, if my mind ever needs blowing, I'll be sure to find myself a Cherokee," I mumble back, awkwardly inching away. "Maybe Lanier and I will see you there." Suddenly, feeling the need to white lie my way out of it, I add "If we don't have a 'thing' we have to go to, we might already have a 'thing' this weekend. Lanier keeps our social calendar, sooo... I'll let you know." Grant winks and gives me a thumbs-up and his card. All nervous-like, I take it and jam it quickly into my pocket. Before I can walk off, an empathetic Rainbow smiles and gives me a 'you-look-like-you-could-use-a-hug' hug.

I search the party for Lanier. I can't wait to tell him about my first encounter with the local wildlife. The Cherokees? Sexperts? Really? I mean, shouldn't I have heard about this before? Read something? Seen something on the History Channel? Why hasn't Ken Burns ever done a documentary about this red-hot tribe? The Cherokees have been around a long time, surely by now, a colorful reference to their legendary sexual prowess would have worked its way into the vernacular like "Me and the Mrs. fucked last night like two Cherokees." But nope, nothing. Not a word. Well... you know what they say... it's always the quiet ones, isn't it? Now, I don't know if it was the altitude or the alcohol, but when I finally find Lanier and tell him the details of my intriguing encounter, his immediate response is "I say let's do it. Isn't that why we moved up here? To experience new things?" "Well, when you put it that way..." He's right, of course. He usually is. The next morning I phone Grant and tell him to count us in. In what? I have no idea.

That Friday night, we arrive at the hilltop home of a wealthy anesthesiologist who is casually dressed in a tee shirt and sweats. He's got a beautiful multicolored peace sign tattooed on one arm, and silver and turquoise Indian bracelets on both his wrists. He couldn't be more welcoming. From a plaque awarded to him by Cedar-Sinai Hospital that is hanging behind him on his foyer wall, I deduce his name is Dr. Alfred Rappaport, but when he introduces himself to us, he uses his Indian name, Running Bear. I assume that's how he's spelling it...or is it Running Bare? I am too uptight to ask. He leads us into a sunken living room lit mostly by candles. There is sexy Indian drumming playing softly in the background and couples are scattered around the living room, many of them already sitting cross-legged on the carpeted floor. Colorful Indian rugs hang on the walls as well as the occasional bleached out animal skull. There is one shelved wall filled with Indian artifacts and Kachina dolls. This guy is really into Navajobilia, or Hopiana or just has a bad case of Cherokeeitis. I don't know and I don't want to know- I just want to leave. Too late. Grant and Rainbow are waving us over. I introduce Lanier who plops right down and starts chatting away with them. I don't feel comfortable sitting on the floor. What if I need to make a run for it!? Instead, I sit down on a brown suede love seat with a woolen Indian blanket thrown decoratively over the back. At both ends of it are two brown wicker side tables with glass tops, on which matching red lava lamps are percolating. I stare anxiously at the lamps with their suggestive blobs of God-only-knows-what floating around inside them. The Catholic schoolboy in me is reawakened. What had Sister Mary Joseph taught us about lava lamps? Oh, yeah… "Lava lamps are the lamps the Devil uses to light the road to Hell." I had laughed back then but now, sitting in the semi-darkness with a bunch of strangers about to receive The Sweet Medicine Sundance Teachings of the Chuluaqui-Quodoushka, it didn't seem so funny.

To my surprise, though the sex teachings seem far out at first; they actually make a lot of sense. Among the Cherokees, there was a sacred sex educational rite of passage for both teenage boys and girls when they reached adolescence. An older member of the tribe called the Fireman or Firewoman would basically explain the facts of life to these teens. This would include a session in the nude where the Fireman would explain to the girls how to please a man, while a Firewoman in a separate teepee, also naked, would explain the workings of the female body to boys and how to plea-sure a woman. All this may sound a little too graphic an approach to the birds and the bees for some of you; but think back to what your parents told you about sex, if anything. When I asked my dad if there was anything I should know about sexual intercourse, he did a spit-take and sprayed beer all over both of us, then sputtered, "Why are you asking *me*?" I took that as a hint that I should get this information instead from my mother. I approached her once while she was relaxed and darning socks. She put down her sewing and looked around like there were spies possibly listening at the door and then whispered, "Just be careful... you can catch things down there", nodding in the direction of my crotch. "What things?" I asked, lost. "I'll say no more..." was her melodramatic, ominous response. That was it. That was all the preparation I was given by those two for one of the most important human interactions I was to have for the rest of my life. Now look where I am, in a stranger's dark, creepy living room for a weekend of crazy, sexed-up sexy Indian sex stuff. If I end up covered in bear grease and whore-paint pulling a train bound for Orgyville this weekend, at least I'll know who to blame.

Bright and early the next day, all fourteen couples of us meet for a perfectly normal chit-chatty getting-to-know-each-other breakfast where some share photos of their kids or talk about their dog or share their upcoming Fourth of July barbecue plans. I almost forget why we are here until a Tibetan gong is struck by Running Bear and we are called into the living room, now with folding chairs set up in rows, for a lecture on different Cherokee classifications of penises and vaginas. According to the Cherokees, a man's member, depending on its size and width, puts a man into one of five anatomical categories. Running bear nonchalantly walks over to the easel and flings it open to a chart. Now normally, I can't stay awake very long for any kind of chart nonsense; too many years of boring, clueless bad teachers. But, this chart has five penises on it! I giggle immediately and Lanier elbows me. Several heads turn in my direction to give me 'oh-grow-up' looks, which I pretend not to notice.

Running Bear starts with the shortest, thinnest, smallest penis, which the Cherokees called 'Coyote Man', then goes on to a short, thick penis called a 'Bear Man' (I try very hard to keep from letting my eyes wander down to Running Bear's running shorts). Then it's on to a medium long, medium thick penis called 'Dancing Man', followed by a long penis that was medium thick in circumference called 'Deer Man', and finishing with the last and most certainly not the least, the longest and thickest ramrod on the reservation called 'Horse Man'. "Any questions?" I start to raise my hand, but Lanier gives me a bug-eyed don't-you-dare look. All I was going to ask was if the size of the horseshoes were any reliable indication of what might be waiting in the barn.

The moment luckily passes and Running Bear flips over to the next chart. I squint my eyes and say "Huh?" (Apparently a little too loudly) "What on earth are those?" I whisper to Lanier. "Vaginas!!!" he whispers back through gritted teeth, mortified. "Well, they don't look like vaginas," I mutter defensively. "You would know, you're the expert!" he shoots back sarcastically. "I was in a vagina once" I protest. "Your mother doesn't count," he whispers, furious.

"Oh," I say, sulking. "Is there a problem?" I hear Running Bear asking. I scan the crowed sympathetically to see who else is having a problem with the vagina chart. I mean, really, the artist who drew them is not in the least bit gifted. "Is there a problem?" he repeats, this time louder. Oh, shit. He's talking to me. "Uh, I can't really see all that well from back here. The nuns were right… too much masturbating and you go blind." I laugh feebly, and there are a few titters here and there. But none from Lanier, who is justifiably staring down at the floor trying to bore a hole into which he can disappear. Some nice lady in the front row, changes places with me and I am now eye to eye with the chart. Bring on the girls... They are Deer Woman with the most petite vagina and easiest to achieve orgasm.... then Sheep Woman ... she's got a long smooth hood over her clitoris. Followed by Buffalo Woman ...She's got the widest, shallowest, wettest vagina of all! (You go girl!) After her, is Wolf Woman with large thin protruding inner lips and last comes... Dancing Woman. That gal's got the largest distance between her clitoris and her vagina and takes the longest to achieve orgasm. That's probably why on this chart; she comes last! There is a lot more talk about labias, clitorises, and other female parts and the pleasuring of them Cherokee style to get to the big 'O'; however I don't take a lot of notes during this part figuring, let's face it, I don't need it for future reference.

When the pee break is finally announced, we all head for the restrooms. While stuck in line for the bathroom, I deliberately do not dare look down, only up at people's faces. The size and shape of every man's penis in the seminar is circling my brain. Look at the women, Terry... the women! A large gal in stretch pants leaving the restroom smiles at me. I bet anything she's got a big, brown buffalo grazing down there. Oh, Jeez- cut it out! I force myself to make distracting small talk with the man in front of me. "I don't believe we've met. I'm Terry." "Oh hey, nice to meet you. I'm Dick." That was no help. Good God, how do you turn this stuff off?

Back from the break, our seminar leader takes us out to his huge, lush, overgrown backyard; on opposite sides of a clearing now stand two very large teepees. Apparently we are to be divided into two groups: men in one teepee and women in the other. Looking at me and raising his eyebrows quizzically, Running Bear says, "We've never had a gay couple take Quodoushka... I'd gladly put you both in the men's tent, but you'll miss out on the valuable dialogue that goes on in the women's tent. So maybe one of you might want to..." He leaves the question hanging in mid-air. Lanier is way in the back of the group but I can feel him willing me not to turn around to ask which one of us is the squaw. "I'd be delighted to go to the women's tent." I chirp cheerily, secretly envisioning juicy gossip, a case of white wine and packs and packs of Marlboro Lights.

Once inside the lady teepee, I see no such amenities, instead, they are serving some kind of Cherokee herb tea that helps with cramps when you're having your period. It tastes to me like somebody boiled an old moccasin. I pretend to sip politely but even the smell of that hot mess is making me queasy. Maybe that's how it works. You're so nauseous; you forget you've got cramps.

The flap of the tent is suddenly flipped open and a thin, waspy blonde comes striding in. Whoever she is, she's traded in her Lily Pulitzer sundress for jeans and a simple white scoop-neck top with tiny white-beaded fringe at the ends of her short sleeves. Instead of the tasteful strand of pearls you'd expect, she is sporting feather earrings and a beaded headband. Before she even says her name, I'm guessing she's a Millicent... a Tiffany... maybe a Constance... here; she introduces herself by her Indian name... Falling Star. Running Bear... Falling Star... Does every Caucasian who teaches about Indian culture feel the need to take on a fake Indian name? What Indian name would I pick, I wonder? 'Sits to Pee'? Too embarrassing. Wait a minute, I know– 'Deer Abbey'? I could have my very own Indian advice column.

Uh oh... time to concentrate. Falling Star's asking all us girls about our sex life. What was the biggest surprise for us on our wedding night? The young lady next to me shoots her hand up. "Yes? Please stand," requests Falling Star politely. "Okay," says she, "like everybody here, I suppose, I'd been raised on tales of Prince Charming, Romeo and Juliet, and Sleeping Beauty being awakened by the kiss of her true love. What nobody prepared me for was the sight of a man's wrinkled balls!" From the entire teepee rise cries of anguish and revulsion. "The scrotum! Yuck!" yells an older woman like she'd seen far too many dingle dangles in her lifetime. There is total mumbled disgust on all sides. Then remembering there is a man in the room, a polite few feel pressured to say "Sorry... but c'mon" or "hey, you gotta admit it's not attractive." "Well, it's not my best feature," I say totally sympathetic. "...That would be my blue eyes", hoping to get them thinking about something else instead of the awful shock of an actual set of guy balls staring them in the face. Okay, so it's a surprise to see them for the first time. Maybe someone should have warned them. But would the Mattel Toy Company ever have sold even one Ken doll to young girlies if they had included a life-like mini nutsack? Not from what I'm hearing in this teepee tell-all.

Another woman raises her hand. She is so sweet and soft-spoken that I really have to strain to hear her. "What about when they..." "Could you speak up, sweetie?" asks Falling Star. The woman clears her throat and boldly raises her volume. "WHAT ABOUT WHEN THEY COME IN YOUR FACE?!!" Horrified gasps escape from all the ladies' lips as their own private man-milkshakes come flooding back. The woman behind me chimes in "...AND IT GETS IN YOUR HAIR!!!" All hell breaks loose after that.

I join in on the hen fest, clucking disapprovingly and nodding my head in agreement with all their womanly complaints. Some go on to gripe about how long their husbands take to come when they are performing oral sex on them. "Why do you think they call it a blow job?!" carps one bitter attendee. "Let's cleanse the energy in this teepee," says Falling Star who looks like she's had enough. Waving a smoking smudge stick, she hurriedly passes through the crowd and opens the exit flap. I don't know who wants out worse, her or me. Well! I don't think I'm going to bring any of *this* back to the men's teepee. Talk about a tough room! As soon as I can, I rush out with a bunch of the wilder ladies and we end up holing up in Dr. Rappaport's guest bedroom where we gossip, drink wine and smoke Marlboro Lights.

Later that night, led by Running Bear and Falling Star, we all gather under the stars and do a Fire Breath Ritual and then share what we've learned, followed by drumming and dancing in the moonlight. The women dance first to seduce the men, and then the men dance next to seduce the women. There's something beautiful and primitive about it. So much so that all of us get naked and stay that way the rest of the night. Even me. It's weird... somehow this crazy Quodoushka has gotten to me. I feel a momentary acceptance of my naked body... no guilt... no shame... accepting and accepted by this group of naked strangers. I look down at my you-know-what. What would the Cherokees classify me? Just then a naked, smiling Grant comes by. "Hi, Terry... told you you'd love this." "You were right..." I smile back and can't help but notice his massive equine Mr. Ed dong swaying in the breeze. I look back down at mine. Well... I can definitely rule out 'Horse Man', but that's okay. Sitting naked, under this beautiful old oak tree out here in the wild tonight; I couldn't be happier.

Escape from HELL.A.

After our lease runs out on our storybook cabin in the wilds of Topanga; we are unfortunately back living in the hard heart of L.A. Ultimately, it was too much of a commute to our city job via a highly dangerous winding canyon road (Topanga Canyon Boulevard) that was heavily dotted with improvised funeral wreaths, homemade white crosses, and morbid memorabilia from motorists and motorcyclists who never made it to their ultimate destination; unless we're talking Heaven. I was always petrified driving home on that scary road at night. I looked like a deer in the headlights taking those curves. I know because there were actual deer in my headlights with my same expression on their faces.

So here we are in December trying bravely to keep our Christmas spirit alive in palm-tree lined sweltering La-la land. Screw it. No matter what, I'm getting us a giant Christmas tree and buying enough ropes of trashy colored-lights to cause a citywide blackout. Before I know it, I'm even breaking out the artificially cinnamon-scented pine cones (even though one whiff of them out of their plastic bag always gives me an instant migraine and one memorable Christmas: head to toe hives…What the hell is on those things?!) Risking my life further, I ignore the dire respiratory warnings on the red and green aerosol fake snow can, and spray toxic carcinogenic fake snow on all my windows. It's 88 degrees outside and I'm very aware that passersby will most likely feel sorry for me like I'm some sad sad Christmas-lovin' loser. But I don't care. (I just hope that's not the fumes from the fake snow talking) I pray I haven't crossed the line into Christmas kookdom. You know who I'm talking about. They leave their decorations out all year… even the lighted giant plastic Santa's sleigh pulled by life-size reindeer on their roof. I'm familiar with the holiday demons they're battling; so I try not to judge. But sometimes you can't help it; once, in July, I saw a hand painted banner still hanging off the second story of some poor soul's house with 'SANTA DIED FOR YOUR SINS' scrawled across it.

Anyway, heads up Hollywood! I'm all ready to get my Christmas on. And soon enough, my first two L.A. Christmas cards are in my mailbox. See…"if you decorate, cards will come." It's the unwritten rule of the yule no matter where you live. The first one is from my next-door neighbor, a middle-aged realtor who nods and waves to me over the fence on his way out of the house to his car and on the way back into his house; but never ever has said an actual word to me. Never. I've had numerous speculative discussions (more than Lanier would probably care to remember) about whether he's deaf, autistic or doesn't speak English. Especially after I've called out trite easy-to-answer suburban inanities like… "Back from the salt mines?" (Work cliché) … and "Would you call this smog or toxic fog?" (Lame weather humor) and my bottom of the barrel manly icebreaker…"Nice car, is it good on gas?"… And received only a silent nod and wave for my trouble.

But now, here I am, holding in my hand, a red envelope with a cute candy-cane stamp on it from this manbot. Awwwww… maybe I've misread my neighbor fella. Maybe he's the painfully shy type that keeps it all bottled up inside. I anxiously tear open the envelope, knowing from past experience; the first card sets the tone for the entire holiday. Inside is a bland-looking dreary drudge of a card with a generic politically correct 'Season's Greetings' on the front. I open it to read some sentiment he has actually taken the time to hand write…"Thank-you for raising property values!" (A vague reference no doubt to the boxwood hedge I planted out front which may have inexplicably added a dollar or so to the asking price of his house next door, should he choose to sell.) 'Thank you for raising property values'? That's it? That's not exactly my idea of a warm and fuzzy kick-off to my holiday. I open my front door and peek out. There he is heading toward his car. I rush out holding up his card "Thanks for the thought! Have a merry one!" I yell trying to sound full of Christmas cheer, although I'm not really feeling it. His response? A nod and a wave. I'm now definitely leaning toward deaf and too cheap to buy a hearing aid, although I haven't ruled out alien possession.

I'm hoping this second card will save the day. I open it with a kind of my-luck's-gotta-change desperation usually reserved for fixed-income retirees in Vegas who've gambled away their Social Security check and are just about to pull the lever on a slot machine that better deliver. But instead of three red cherries, my jackpot card's got three porky pre-teens in identical cherry-red Christmas sweaters on its cover. Who in God's name are these children? Do I know their parents? If so, where are they? Did these three kill 'em and eat 'em? "Merry Christmas from Brian, Christy and Mary Jo!" Who?!!!

Okay, this is the height of L.A. kid-centric nonsense. I'm not their kids' friend; I'm their friend, whoever they are. Shouldn't their faces be somewhere on this thing? This reeks of that sanctimonious baby-on-board trend that was so popular years ago. A clear message that because someone's child is on board; I should drive with extra special caution around them. The thinking behind that I presume being their baby's life is worth more than any mature adult on the road like you or me. This kid could be the future President of the United States…You? You've probably already peaked… what else are we going to get outta you? Why don't I just put a sign on my car's back window that says "No child on board… so it's ok to hit me!"

It's pretty obvious this second card is not doing much to put me in the holiday mood. These two Christmas clunkers are not good omens. As a matter of fact, now I'm scared. I fasten my seat belt. It looks like this holiday's going to be a bumpy sleigh ride from here on in. Or is it? I get an exciting email later that week from an actor friend of mine. He's forwarded me a breakdown from a television-casting agent asking for a 'Terry Sweeney type'. Christmas is here early!!! Okay, now we're talking. Forget the mercenary real estate appraisal card; tell Brian, Christy and Mary Jo to go stuff a stocking … someone in Hollywood is looking for ME!!! I call immediately thinking how thrilled they'll be to hear that Terry Sweeney himself is on the line. No one else need apply. As the phone rings, I think to myself; don't ask for too much… don't hold the network hostage… after all they've probably been searching the country for you. A young lady answers the phone…"Hello?" "Is Tony (the casting agent) there? Terry Sweeney calling." "Who?" she asks. "Terry Sweeney…your boss is looking for me!" "Uh… hold on." I hear her mention my name and mad mumbling back and forth. No doubt the casting office is abuzz with this stroke of good luck… If only they were all this easy. A male voice comes on the line "Terry…Tony." "Hey, Tony! Sooooo, you're looking for a Terry Sweeney type… Well here I am. Look no further… and the good news is I'm available." "Yes… well," clearing his throat, "the thing is we're looking for a

Terry Sweeney type…" "Yes, and I'm the real Terry Sweeney. You're looking for me." "Actually, we're looking for someone like you but a younger version of you." "But I still look the same… really! You know how they say 'black don't crack', well in my case… beige don't age!" "Yeah…that's funny…anyway… thanks for calling, Terry. I'm a big fan." CLICK!!! (Cut to: A HIGH-PITCHED SCREAM EMANATING FROM MY CALIFORNIA BUNGALOW THAT CAN BE HEARD IN A REMOTE VILLAGE AT THE FOOT OF MACCHU PICCHU.)

I'm reminded of an article. I once read in a Psychology Today magazine that talked about an experiment where frogs were put in a pan of delightfully warm water and the water's temperature was raised ever so slowly. The frogs never even tried to jump out because they didn't realize they were being boiled alive. Is that what's happening to me floating out here in warm sunny-day-in and sunny-day-out L.A.? Maybe it's time; I jump out of this pot. I've had this feeling before. Who hasn't sat in their cubicle, a virtual prisoner to their company's computer thinking about making 'The Great Escape'? Once, Lanier and I, after our one-hundredth showbiz belly punch, went so far as flying to Colorado and looking at an elk ranch we saw for sale on line. Sounds crazy I know but reserve judgment till you hear the facts. Elk shed their horns once a year. That's right; they just fall off. Simple as that. So what if a person, say me, could just stroll along behind them picking their horns up and carting them off to the barn where another person, say Lanier, could grind them into a powder. Why would we do that, you ask? Because Japanese men consider ground elk horn to be a major aphrodisiac… capable of making their wee wees unfailingly rock hard for hours and hours. That's right! Japanese Viagra! Worth a fortune! And we don't need a patent or even a medical degree! (Although I did think of making it sound doctor-approved with the possible name of 'DR. HORNY'S AMAZING LOVE-YOU-LONG-TIME POWDER')

So there we were, way outside of Boulder, touring the 25-acre ranch we saw on realtor.com with some chatty country bumpkin realtor. As he small-talked us up one side and down the other; our eyes caught sight of a huge herd of elk roaming our future property... that was it; we were ready to make an offer, right then and there. We'd even picked out our home's future name... "TWO FAGS RANCH." We figured that's what our macho cowboy neighbors would call it so we might as well beat 'em to it. We imagined them giving directions to folks... "Oh... you're looking for the Costco? Well, just go straight down this here road till you hit TWO FAGS RANCH and make a right and keep going, you can't miss it."

It seemed we'd hit upon the perfect escape; but turned out there were a few chinks in the armor of this easy get-rich-quick scheme I hadn't counted on. For one thing, the smell of the elk herd... a combination of boiled road kill and rotting sewage that made me gag. Secondly was the bleak, lonely creepy vibe of the ranch house itself. Touring the inside of it with the real estate agent, I caught a glimpse of a water glass on a windowsill with somebody's false teeth still in it. "Somebody left in an awful hurry...Murder or suicide?" I asked jokingly. The realtor's eyes bugged out and he snapped defensively, "Who have you been taking to?!" "Uh...nobody... nobody at all," I answered quickly. He abruptly changed the subject and his menacing tone..."let's take another look at that barn, shall we boys?" Lanier and I practically raced him out the door.

Outside a large fluffy snowflake landed on my shoulder. Snow?! In the first week of September? Wait a minute...snow! "September, October, November, December, January, February, March and

April?... And sometimes May..." confessed the realtor. I imagine Lanier and I snowed in that morbid crime scene for nine months out of the year. How long before I got into the ground elk horn?! "His penis seems to have exploded... that's the only explanation I can come up with..." the coroner would say, "Weird... same thing that killed the old man who owned this place before him."

So of course, we didn't buy it. Back to present time, I could have happily lived my entire life without hearing that I can't even get an acting job playing myself. This is the last straw... Where's Lanier? I seem to say that at every crossroads and crisis that has popped up since the day we met. I can't help it. He's one of the smartest men I know. The thing about my beautiful Southern-born hubby is he's a true Renaissance man. Lanier knows something about everything: art, architecture, history, food, fashion, biodynamic gardening, transcendentalism and more importantly how to handle a high-strung horse like myself. The man's amazing. He can tell you how to identify telltale marks on a shard of ancient pottery one minute, how to root a begonia the next and minutes later, what new contemporary artist's cutting edge show is up at the coolest gallery in Berlin. But what I love most about my very own Ashley Wilkes is that he's got such innate high integrity. So much so that on occasion when a show biz deal's gotten uncomfortable and artistically compromising; he has honestly said "Let's give 'em back the money." (Too bad the Scarlet in me has already spent it!). Lanier loves the South... it's in his blood and in his heart...and I know he would love to go back there. It is I who have insisted we stay here in this L.A. rat race and try to score the next big hunk of cheese. But today was one rat too many.

I don't have to say a word. When I find him in his office; he's on Realtor.com again, this time looking at a photo of 'Bythewood', a beautiful, historic antebellum house for sale in Beaufort, South Carolina; a romantic coastal town between Charleston and Savannah. "What would you say to flying back there and spending Christmas in the Low country?" he asks smiling mischievously. "Done!" I decree. I need my Christmas moved somewhere else and fast. This year, I am taking Santa to the *South* Pole. We don't know it yet, but we two frogs are about to jump out of the pot.

South of Crazy

Beaufort is such a beautiful, magical small southern town, I immediately feel like I've stepped back in time. Maybe for the better…
maybe not. Our first day here, I remember asking someone where
the Starbucks was. "Well…" she answered, "you go down to that
corner and take a left, then go a couple of miles and make a right
and there it is…" "The Starbucks?" "No," she said, "the on ramp
for Route 17… just stay on it for two hours till you hit Charleston.
There's one there." No Starbucks?! No kidding. No wonder my
liberal L.A. friends were horrified when they heard I'd just bought
a house here. I'm sure they envisioned angry Christian mobs in
camouflage surrounding the place chanting "Adam and Eve, not
Adam and Steve!" But instead, Lanier and I are greeted like a pair
of visiting pandas from China. We're an instant hit. "I'm having
the gays for lunch!" "The gays are coming to my house for cocktails
this Saturday!" "Well, I'll have you know the gays are coming to
my house the following day to see my roses!" Our dance card is so
full we have to double and triple book. I drank so much that first
week down here; I thought I was going to have to put my name
on a waiting list for a new liver. So much for the bad rap the Red
States get. All you need in the South to get by is charm, good
manners, and be able to tell a good story (and hold your liquor!!!)

But now that I think about it, there's one more thing you have to get used to living in a small southern town… the gossip gets home before you do.

A realtor informs me that the old lady down the street, Cornelia, is the worst gossipmonger in Beaufort. "Get ready!!! She'll be here within the week. Whatever you do, don't let her in," she solemnly warns me. As she leaves, she points in the direction of an innocent-looking, cutesy cottage with pink shutters. "It lives there, and chances are it's already seen us. Lock the door behind me." With that, she scrambles down my back stairs and roars off in her Chevy Tahoe. Southerners are such drama queens, I remember thinking. These are after all, the gals who invented the vapors and the hissy fit.

The next morning, there's a knock at my door, and when I open it, there is the sweetest, grey-haired little old lady with two pink oven mitts holding a loaf pan. "Hello, darlin'," she coos "Welcome to Beaufort… this is my famous orange-lemon pound cake… it's just hot out of the oven. I'd better put it in your kitchen myself." And with that she hustles past me before I can get out a word of protest. "Well, the kitchen is…" "Oh, I know where it is, dear. I know every house on this block inside and out and where all the bodies are buried," she says with a sly smile. This has got to be Cornelia. What the hell have I done?! I look for my phone to try and text someone to call me with a fake emergency so I can get her out of here, but no luck. I can hear her bustling around in my kitchen and as I peek around the corner, I see the pound cake on the stove and the two mitts hastily abandoned alongside it. She is looking at the backs of the china I was unpacking and then goes on to lift the lid on my box of silver. She stares at the pattern like a professional appraiser. I clear my throat and say "Let me guess, you're Cornelia." She nods coyly, "Guilty." "I'm Terry, and upstairs that's my friend Lanier you hear unpacking boxes." At the word *friend*, a small jaded smile plays at the corners of her mouth as if to say "Friend? Yeah, right. I already know you two are raging homosexuals from L.A." Her head swivels around from one room to the other wondering, no doubt, which one we're going to use for our orgies. To distract her I ask, "Did you know Mary Potter well?" (Mary Potter being the old lady who had lived in our house for a gazillion years.) Despite the fact we'd bought the house and our names were on the deed; everybody we'd met so far in Beaufort continues to say, "Oh, you're living in Mary Potter's house." Like even though she's dead as a doornail, she still owns it and always will. "Mary Potter was my dear, dear friend, says Cornelia a little too sweetly… now you didn't hear this from me, but when she died, she left orders in her will to have Tabasco, her mean one-eyed old cat put to sleep and buried with her. I haven't heard that done since the Phay-rohs." "No, I didn't know that…" I answer politely. "And bless her heart, I love her to death, but I'd never call her a generous person, oh, no, you'd never call her that… she'd walk ten miles to put a letter in someone's mailbox rather than buy a postage stamp. Oh, my Lawd, they didn't come any cheaper." "I think the nice word for it is frugal." I say, trying not to speak ill of the dead just in case her penny-pinching ghost is still hanging around.

I start to move towards the front door. "This has been very edifying…" Little did I know Cornelia was just getting warmed up. For the next half hour came a breathless flash flood of rumors and innuendo about everyone in the neighborhood. I could barely keep up with all the names but every so often I would hear "… of course, they could never *prove* he did it…" Did what? Murder? Rape? Robbery? "Have you met the Oswalds down the street yet?

The wife's a friend o' mine… bless her heart she's nice but plain as a mud fence… husband's a skirt chaser and the biggest drunk in town… even named his boat 'Cirrhosis of the River'. Maybe if she got that lazy eye of hers fixed, she'd see he's sleeping with the babysitter… she's the daughter of the doctor who cut off the wrong leg." On and on… "See that new house just went up on the corner?" "Oh, yes… beautiful," I chirp honestly. "Cocaine money!!!" She sniffs, holding one nostril closed and pantomiming doing a line of blow. Now I'm scared… I gotta get her out of here. I push the front door open and bow, acting like a good old-fashioned southern gentleman. She smiles flirtatiously as if she were eighteen instead of eighty and on her way out pauses momentarily to gaze at a mahogany sideboard in my dining room. "Did you get this here?" asks Cornelia. "No… At an antiques store in Charleston" I answer, and then add proudly "It's eighteenth century." She looks at me smiling, "Think so? Bless your heart, they saw you coming." Before I know it, the witch is outside the front door, just about to descend the front steps, when she suddenly whirls around and flutters her eyes innocently. "Can I ask you a question?"

Oh, Lord… she's about to put the cheese in the mousetrap. Careful, Terry… "Yes, of course," I smile back nervously. "Are you independently wealthy?" As she waits for my answer, I can almost see the old cat twirling her whiskers. "Of course not." I tell her truthfully, "We both have to work for a living." "Of course, you do…" She smiles ever so smugly and takes off down the stairs. Over her shoulder she shouts, "I'll be back one of these days for that loaf pan, don't you worry…" "I CAN BRING IT TO YOU!!! I'LL LEAVE IT ON YOUR PORCH!!!" I yell back a little too loudly. Once she is outside my gate, a wave of relief washes over me. Well, I got through that.

Within a week of her visit though, I start hearing there is a rumor flying around Beaufort that Lanier and I are 'Hollywood millionaires'. Of course, if I had claimed I was loaded, she most likely would have gone around telling everyone "I don't believe those two phonies have a pot to piss in." Now, it may sound on the surface, like it's better to have people thinking you're rich, but suddenly every contractor, painter, plumber, and electrician in the county, who comes to give us an estimate, starts them at $5,000.00, no matter what it's for. "I can switch out that doorknob for say...$5,000.00." "You know that clogged toilet in your downstairs bathroom? For $5,000.00 I can get a plunger and..." What had that woman brought upon us? As I ponder my options and thumb through the Yellow Pages seeking out-of-town contractors, I hear Cornelia on the street. I peek out the blinds. She's down below at our side gate with another old gal. I hear the dear old thing remark sweetly to Cornelia, "What a beautiful garden they have." Well now ... I swell up with pride thinking to myself... at least all the man-hours and blood, sweat, and tears, not to mention backbreaking weeding, raking, and planting, are finally being appreciated. It's then I hear Cornelia sniff "All it takes is money."

***

Anyway, that explains how we got involved with a redneck contractor from Ridgeland, a couple of towns over. Cornelia's gossip had not gone beyond Beaufort's city limits, thank God. So when Big Ed Rayburn's modest quote came in to repair all four of our fireplaces, Lanier and I jumped at it.

When Big Ed shows up on day one to begin the work, he has his trained assistant, Dennis with him. At least that's who I imagine he is. Turns out he's Big Ed's future son-in-law, as Big Ed explains it to us, "I'm breaking the boy into the remodeling biz… he's gotta start somewhere, y'all." This is an 18th century house on the National Historic Register. You're telling me this 19-year-old gap toothed high school dropout fiancé of your daughter, who looks like he parts his brick red bushy hair with an ax, is going to learn from his mistakes on my barely paid for antiquated, southern mansionette? I don't think so. Lanier and I excuse ourselves for a minute so that we might have an emergency mini-conference. Lanier is shaking his head 'no', but as I glance over at Big Ed's giant bare arm, I see that it's covered in tattoos that tell the story of his life in blue and black ink. The first (the oldest and most faded) is of barbed wire that circles his wrist. Above that is a tattoo of dice; above that, a very slutty-looking naked lady; above that a Hell's Angel logo over a motorcycle and at the tippy-top is his most recent tattoo in bright blue, −one word: JESUS. Big Ed can see we're getting cold feet. "I'll supervise, don't you worry none!" We decide to take a chance. Winter is coming and we want to have wood fires going when it gets here. "Alright, Big Ed, have at it!" I shout confidently, but inside I'm singing "Jesus Take the Wheelbarrow" and keep those two from screwing this up.

So off they start on the demolition of my delicate circa 1792 fireplaces by first removing what needs to be carted off. I tiptoe upstairs to spy on Dennis the Red Menace who, unsupervised, is robotically swinging a sledgehammer as though in a trance; I swear I saw him drooling. Oh, dear Lord, I can't watch this.

Downstairs, Big Ed has his head stuck up my dining room chimney. Withdrawing it slowly, he sits back on his haunches scratching his head, perplexed and mumbling "Damn" to himself. Like he's never seen the inside of a chimney before in his life. That's it. I run out the front door and pull on my garden gloves. I head for my roses to cut a dozen or so to make a bouquet.

Before long, the young rebel rooster comes out for a cigarette break. Why not? He's been working a good fifteen minutes. Time to break out the Marlboros. Seeing me out in the yard, he scoots toward me puffing away on his cigarette. "You play video games?" "Uh, yes, I have on occasion", I lie. "Ever play 'Death Dealer'?" "No…" I say slowly, "…I don't think so." I'm a gay guy on my knees with pale chartreuse garden gloves on that I ordered from William Sonoma, gathering long-stemmed roses to put in a lovely sterling silver vase. Do I look like I play Death Dealer? "You won't believe how many people you can kill in just one sittin'. I killed about a thousand the other day… ten thousand and you're officially on the Death Dealer VIP Death Squad." I am finding this conversation <u>very</u> painful. How long is he going to smoke that cigarette? Has this redheaded wrecking ball forgotten he's got a 200-year-old fireplace to smash to smithereens? As if reading my thoughts, he turns around to go back in but stops remembering he was supposed to be on a mission "Oh, uh… Ed wants to talk to the owner of the house." "We both own the house," I tell him casually "so he can talk to both of us." He knits his big fuzzy red eyebrows together totally confused "You <u>both</u> own the house <u>together</u>?" Suddenly, I see a dim, 15-watt bulb light up in his thick red head. "Oh?" Oh…"OH!" When he skedaddles back in to report this astonishing bit of news, I decide to follow him, curious to see what Big Ed's reaction will be. Breathing heavily with excitement, he rushes up to Big Ed, whose head is still stuck up the chimney "Ed! Ed! They <u>both</u> own the house." "What?!" I hear a muffled yell from inside the chimney. "They <u>both</u> own the house." Ed sticks his head back out into the open and stares at his apprentice bewildered… "They <u>both</u>…? Oh? Oh…OH!" They look from one to another, eyes wide with terror: H-O-M-O-S-E-X-U-A-L-S… I can see the neon sign flashing on and off in their backwoods brains.

I slip into the room holding my fresh-picked bouquet in my green-gloved hands. "Did you want to ask me something, Ed?" "Oh, no…no…no…no…I'm fine…fine…just fine…" he stammers. "Well, don't hesitate if you need anything… I'm all yours!" I add with a wink. That last bit makes him drop his flashlight. I notice the rest of the day; they work feverishly…as though they need to quickly be done with these chimneys before they inhale any more fairy dust.

Finally, within the week, the work is done. Somehow my chimneys are still standing and the fireplaces appear to be intact and working. Now Ed had said he was charging me $400.00 a fireplace for the four. When I hand him a check for $1,600.00, I say, "It's an out-of-state check. I hope that's okay." Says Ed "Hmm…Lemme see." He reads it out loud…"City National Bank of BEVERLY HILLS!?!?!" The words 'Beverly Hills' are shouted so loudly I'm sure the bank teller back in L.A. could hear it. Practically shaking, he mumbles something or other, jumps in his truck and peels out. Five minutes later he's knocking on my front door. "Yes?" I ask him. "When I told you it was $400.00 a fireplace… well that day I had a bad sinus headache and I didn't know what I was sayin'. You know, the pills they give you make you so damn fuzzy… Uh… it's $600.00 a fireplace." Really? This Hee-Haw hick is hustling me for $800.00 more. I look over my shoulder at my big white wooden house. It wouldn't take more than a homicidal half-witted future son-in-law and a can of gas to torch it. I look Big Ed in the eye. I know he's lying and he knows he's lying. But he's licking his lips nervously… ready for a fight. "Okay, Big Ed… I'll give you what you say is coming to you." I write a second check knowing it's still less than half of the $5,000.00 quote I got from everyone here in town. When I hand it to him, he takes it and waving his big finger in my face; chides me solemnly "Now you city slickers shouldn't go trying to pull a fast one on a poor country boy like me!" And with that, he jumps back in his pickup and is gone. Huh?! The more time I spend down here in this convoluted land of cotton, the more I find it hard to believe that the South actually lost the war.

THE FRONT YARD FOLLIES

It is a sultry breezy Sunday, one of the first of the summer. The kind of day in early June that knocks on your front door and insists you come outside and play. The coif-busting humidity that can take a normally attractive head of hair and turn it into a sticky damp fur ball that looks like something the cat threw up; hasn't gotten to town yet. So, taking advantage of that, I pour myself an ice-cold glass of wine and meander outside down the old brick path that runs down the middle of our garden. Well... not that it's really that old... it's only been here four months. But it was made to look four hundred years old by a very talented black brick mason whose work I had admired over at one of the black churchyards. Although people threw all kinds of names at me for suggested hires for the job; I was determined to find this man in particular; and finally I did. His name was Rodney Batiste...a streetwise smooth-talker with a mischievous twinkle in his eye. I could tell he was nervous the day he showed up. I soon found out why. He had never been called over to do a big fancy job like this for a white homeowner. The white bricklayers had most of the gigs in the big historic houses sewn up tight. "Well...I told him...There are two reasons I'm hiring you, Rodney... One is because Lanier and I love your work... and two,

I can't stand white people; they get on my nerves." That cracked him up and from that moment on, we hit it off.

But it wasn't as ideal as that may sound. Just because he liked me, didn't mean he wasn't going to take me for a ride. "I'm gonna have this done, Mr. Terry, in six days." (What he meant was sixty.) "I'll need some upfront money, Mr. Terry, for materials, hire a helper and you know this and that and that and this." I pay him half on that very first day, the rest to be paid when he finishes ("See you tomorrow, Mr. Terry!")... Well, first thing, he disappears for two weeks. No calls returned. No calls received. Gone with the wind, baby.

He shows up out of nowhere, at dawn one day, with his helper, Keith, which he pronounces "Keef" who can't stop yawning and looks rather rumpled, like he's just gotten outta bed or hasn't been there yet. Of course, I march indignantly out there since we are already eight days past when he'd said he'd be done. "Oh, Mr. Terry, you won't believe what happened to me... my shoes exploded." "Okay, stop right there. You're absolutely right; I don't believe a word", I shoot back. "But I do believe I'm going to fire you if you pull a no-show like that again. Everyone on the block is watching how you do... don't screw this up!" And back in I march.

The direct approach worked. Next day, he is in my yard, bright and early, measuring and setting the strings in place to make a straight path. He's even brought his big brooding son to help. "He wants to drop outta high school, so I'm gonna have him lay bricks all day with me; a couple of weeks of that and he's gonna run, not walk, back to school and drop all that drop-out bullshit." Very clever... more folks should take their kids to work with them. My father did and that's why I'm not a butcher today... well, that and I'm vegetarian... and gay... and faint at the sight of blood.

I was glad he'd brought the boy since it is obvious, Rodney can use all the help he can get; since "Keef" is only good for about an hour; before he'd climb into Rodney's pick-up to sleep. I had had a sign made up at the printers that read 'Brickwork Being Done by Rodney Batiste, Master Brick Mason' with his telephone number so that he might pick up more jobs at the big houses. Rodney was thrilled with the sign, but I was not thrilled by what I saw next to it- "Keef" snoring in the front seat with his bare feet sticking out the window above it. I pulled Rodney aside. "Rodney, look at that... does it really make a good first impression on potential clients to see 'Keef' sleeping on the job?" Rodney shook his head sympathetically. "You gotta understand somethin', Terry... between the drugs and the liquor and the womens and the stayin' out all night; he tired." I guessed Keef was just a young bachelor sowing his wild oats "I didn't know he was single." I say. "He's not... he's married with fo' kids!"

Anyway, all of January and February, Rodney is outside my door with his eldest son and his burnt-out, exhausted party animal of an assistant, 'Keef'. I make them imported Belgian hot chocolate every morning and swirl whip cream on top. Yeah, I know that sounds a little O.T.T., but I felt guilty... me, in this toasty warm historic plantation house and these poor black guys lugging bricks around in the frigid morning air. My neighbors actually asked me to stop... "What are you doing?! You're ruining it for everyone! You can't spoil your workers like that!" Why not?!... One morning, I come out with the three steaming mugs of chocolate but without the usual topping since I was out of it. The three of them look down at their mugs frowning and then sourly up at me. Rodney, giving me the dirtiest look of the bunch asked, "Where de whip cream?!!"

The last week in February I am nervous about them actually finishing this brick walk during my lifetime; I have a historic house tour I am scheduled to be on, the first of March. Like a mother hen, I hover and cluck. I buy and deliver them lunches. I bake them cookies. Fresh pots of hot coffee are always at the ready. I am like some manic cheerleader for Team Rodney; out on the porch cheering for every brick laid. That's probably how I notice the old 1970s Mercury Marquis rumbling ominously around my block over and over. The driver... a ferocious evil-eyed madwoman who keeps shooting if-looks-could-kill daggers at my front yard. After two days of this, I run up to Rodney to see what the hell this is all about...Rodney takes me aside. "Terry, what is that movie where a man sleeps with a woman and he don't tell her he married and she turns out to be CRAZY?!" "You mean 'Fatal Attraction'?" "That's it!" he says, slapping his thigh. "Hey, Keef!" he yells across the yard, "You gots yo'self a Fatal Attraction!" No. No. Not in my yard, he doesn't. I envision seeing my little pet pug's head sticking out of a pot, boiling away on the stove. "Rodney! For the love of God, please tell Keef from now till Friday the only thing he can lay is bricks!!!"

Somehow, Rodney pulled it off. I gave him a big box of embossed business cards (his first set) as a thank you. And on March first, when the docent from Historic Beaufort took a group of folks down that brick walk, I had to smile when I heard her say "The house was built in 1792 as was this walk; you can see the way the bricks were all hand laid and the path rolls seamlessly with the contours of the land. You won't find that kinds of craftsmanship anymore." Not unless you call Rodney Batiste. Oh, and guess what? The last day he was here, Rodney spilled the secret acid wash solution he used to give the bricks that antiquated look, on his shoes. And what do you know? His shoes started smoking and his toes popped out... I guess you could say his shoes exploded.

***

As I walk out the big wrought-iron gate out front, I leave my fond memories of Rodney behind, and instead take stock of how my dozens of sword ferns and two giant canary palms are faring. I travel back in time once more, thinking about the strange man who took all day delivering the two palms.

"He has a terrible sense of direction, so don't complain to me!" warns the rude saleswoman at the nursery where we had bought them. My first thought was then why did you hire him to be your delivery guy, lady? But, of course, this is the South and one soon learns never to ask a sensible question. Kindly keep your good ol' fashioned Yankee common sense to yourself is the rule. Still, I vainly persist in trying to get this snapping turtle to set up a delivery time before I leave. "Can you call him?" I suggest politely. "His cell phone don't work" is what I get back. "Well, can you print out directions for him from Map Quest?" "Matt Quest? Sorry, don't know him!" What do you say to that?! (I remember I told a waitress in a diner down here that I was lactose intolerant and she said, "I don't like those people either, but I say live and let live.") I give up and Lanier draws on the back of a nursery business envelope a rough sketch of where we are and what are the cross streets, and hands it to her. "We'll be home all day." I assure her. "Makes no difference to me, they're your trees now," she shrugs. Charming! But I suppose when you go to a discount wholesale nursery in the middle of nowhere called 'Shrubs n' Stuff" you don't get Miss Congeniality waiting on you.

We get home and piddle around in the garden, keeping an eye out for a truck with two giant palms tied onto the back of it. Tick tock. Three hours, four hours, five hours... finally he shows up in his camouflage pickup truck with our two trees precariously hanging on for dear life. He gets out slowly and takes a big stretch. He's super tall and skinny as a rail with some teeth here and some teeth there, but none of them touching. "Got lost!" He yells to us as he starts yanking at the big ropes and slashing at them with a bowie knife. These palms are pretty big so Lanier and I offer to help the guy unload them. "No...no...no...Don't you worry. I'm used to lifting heavy shit. My night job is picking up dead bodies." "Excuse me?" I ask, wondering if I've heard right. "You know...if somebody croaks in the middle of the night, I drive out, roll the corpse up in a rubber sheet, pile it into my pickup and take it to the morgue. I tell you though... some of those damn houses on those dark country roads sure are hard to find." I don't believe it! Mr. No-Sense-of-Direction is holding down two delivery jobs! I imagine the poor families who sit in their houses for hours staring at their dead granny's corpse getting colder and stiffer by the minute while this crazy is lost, driving up to the wrong people's house, knocking on their door and scaring the hell out of them announcing "I'm here for your dead body!"

***

But now, six months later, here the palms stand, perfectly framing my front gate. All the sword ferns I had laboriously planted are now a sea of green tendrils waving gently in the breeze. Ah... these could be 'The Southern Gates of Gay Heaven'...I think, sipping my crisp grassy Sauvignon Blanc. From behind me across the street, I hear the gentle raking of my neighbor's pebble driveway by their African-American gardener. He has the timeless Hollywood movie look of the old family retainer. There's even a touch of grey at both his temples. He could be sixty... he could be eighty... all I know about him is he's worked across the street since we moved here. We've seen each other quite frequently, but he is so quiet and reserved that we've never spoken. I take another sip of wine and to my surprise, behind my back I hear him say, "I'd sure like a taste of that." I am happy to finally have the chance to chat with him and turn around... "Oh, I know. A cold glass of wine on a hot day like this really hits the spot." "I don't mean that," he says, pointing at the glass. "I mean *that*" he says, and points his finger at me.

In shock, I automatically utter an embarrassed but polite "thank-you" and turn to leave. "You know..." he continues while coming a little closer, "I've been watching you a looong time..." I flash back to what he's been staring at from his private point of view directly across the street, behind me. Months and months of me bent over, my butt thrusting in and out as I yanked out a gazillion hard-to-budge rooted weeds in front of this gate. "And let me tell you somethin'..." he pauses to look me up and down. "Baby... you make my dick jump!" Dear Lord! In the past, I'd dated my share of guys; both black and white but I'd never heard that one. What is that, pillow talk from prison?! This time I try to be firmer... "I'll have you know that my husband is right in that house and if he knew you were talking to me like this he would be very angry. So I'm just going to go back in that gate and forget we ever had this conversation." And with that, I turn back around to leave. "Okay," he says wistfully, "but you're gonna miss nine inches of memories."

With that, I stumble up my brick steps and yell "I'll be right there, Lanier!" pretending he's been watching protectively and has summoned me from the second floor balcony of our house. He's actually still in bed reading the New York Times and sipping contently on his second Bloody Mary. I take off running and don't stop until I get in my front door. Once inside, I chug my wine, hoping there's still more where that came from. When I've calmed down, I call a good friend of mine who's recently divorced and repeat the entire lewd exchange. She's awfully quiet for a minute, then says "Nine inches of memories, huh? Think you could get me his number?"

THE VIOLIN RECITAL

I open my mailbox one morning to find a hand-written envelope with my name, along with Lanier's, elegantly printed on it. It is from our eighty-eight year old neighbor down the street. Inside on a single piece of notepaper is the following:

> Subject: Violin Recital
> Date: June the 11th (Friday)
> Time: 4:00 PM
> Please do come if you can...

Since when does she play the violin? Or does she have some ancient gramophone she plans to crank up to play some early, scratchy, vintage 1930s recordings of Jascha Heifetz? Or has she gone senile and confused her antique-jammed condo with Carnegie Hall?! Well, whichever it is, we are going. You don't say 'no' to a character like Dottie McDaniels.

I met her one cold winter day, sashaying down the street in a hounds tooth wool cape and a two-toned Sherlock Holmes felt hat with a pheasant feather sticking out of it. As I was introducing myself, she suddenly touched my arm and said, "You have beautiful elocution. Come directly to my home. I want to hear you read all of my favorite poems." So, over I went and read poem after poem from a large scrapbook to her as she sighed and applauded politely to each and every rendition. At the end of my recital, she thanked me ever so sweetly and added in one of her many non-sequiturs, "You know I've had two husbands and they were both named Cecil."

Lanier instantly loved her too and we would pay her surprise visits, dropping off boxes of frozen shrimp scampi (her favorite guilty pleasure) and sharing a bottle of wine. She had recently sold her big old Victorian house and had downsized to a much smaller condo (without giving up one stick of furniture) and was always eager to show off her latest magical reconfiguration of its contents, which usually involved having moved an impossibly heavy Victorian piece of brown furniture from one side of the room to the other. Who helped her? We never found out. But some friendly giant with super strength and even more patience piled her things on top of each other, sometimes to the ceiling. We did, however, help her with the parking lot behind her townhouse, which she wanted to convert into a garden. Before long, dozens and dozens of flower-pots, garden statues and baby boxwoods in tasteful planters filled what used to be the two ugly parking spaces assigned to her. We even got her a great big Chinese Elm so she'd have a bit of shade (SOMEBODY actually busted a hole through the asphalt to bury the tree in the soil below!! WHO??!). She loved it so and called her new asphalt garden her "Sky Room" because she could look up at the clouds by day and the stars by night. There was something delightfully poignant and poetic about her, and we just adored her.

So on the appointed Friday of the recital, we arrive five minutes early on her doorstep with a nice bottle of French cabernet in hand to soften the hard antique chairs that we know await us. To our surprise, her living room is quite packed. All the invitees had probably been as curious as we two. In the middle of the living room is Dottie's large solid oak upright piano, which 'SOMEBODY' (Identify yourself, please!) had moved from a forgotten corner in the room. Seated at it, is a somber, pinch-faced grey haired lady with wire-rim glasses whom I'd never seen around town before this moment. Standing next to her is a tall, hawk-nosed young man with an unruly mass of black curly hair who looks like a mad wild-eyed Siberian refugee and who is clutching his violin like someone here might snatch it and run. Where on earth did she find these two?

I hand Dottie the wine and she distractedly takes it and cradles it like it's an infant. I'm about to say I can open it for her if she has a corkscrew, when the temperamental violinist charmlessly announces in a heavy Slavic accent..."Is time!" Is time? Is time for my wine, buddy. But no, Dottie has already taken her seat and urges us to take the two empty chairs next to her, still cradling the bottle in her arms. We had planned on having a belt or two to get through this. Too late now. The two abruptly strike the opening chords of their living room concert. No pleasantries, no information on what the piece we are about to hear is called or who the hell wrote it. Not even an "I'm Ivan Bitchyurcokoff and I'm Sara Von Sourpuss... welcome one and all." Nope. Off they go...him, morosely staring at his music and her, squinting at hers so hard, you're almost positive she's got the wrong glasses on. They get about two minutes into the piece when an off-key note from one of them causes them to stop. The violinist glares at the pianist, raising a very disturbed bushy black eyebrow in her direction. She, in turn, gives him a dismissive wave of her hand as if to say 'It wasn't me, it was you'. Both, now in a snit, which they barely conceal, return to the first page of their respective sheet music, and begin again without a word of apology for their false start. My mind wanders. Why didn't I bring a wine with a screw cap? At least Lanier and I could be secretly taking hits of it right out of the bottle when no one was looking. Oh, hell.

The piece drags on and on. The violinist is sweating and staring so anxiously at his music, he looks like he's playing in front of a firing squad. Miss Personality, at the piano, frowns disgustedly every time she turns to a new page like some juvenile delinquent broke into her house last night and scribbled 'Bite Me!" on every sheet of her music.

On and on, this fugue drones seemingly without end. Suddenly, Dottie's old rotary phone rings. And rings. And rings. When you're eighty-eight, you give yourself plenty of time to get that pesky old telephone- no sense breaking a hip for a wrong number. On it rings. The two musicians look at each other incensed that this lowly contraption dares to interrupt their highbrow concerto. Dottie is oblivious–the only one in the room apparently that can't hear that phone. Finally, after what I count to be fifteen long piercing rings, Dottie's old-fashioned answering machine picks up. Naturally, due to her age-impaired hearing, its volume is turned up as high as it will go. "Dottie... it's Fanny... I am so sorry I am calling at the last minute to inform you that I am unable to attend your musical event. But, as you know, I have recently been to the doctor about my bladder..." The violinists and the pianist, both furious, have raised the volume and intensity of their playing to compensate for this rudest of interruptions. He now looks like he's sawing a branch off a dead oak and she is beating the piano's ivories like they're still attached to the elephant.

"My doctor, Dr. Gambrell, he's the nephew of Arthur Gambrell, the insurance man whose wife thought she was pregnant but it turned out to be a ten-pound tumor the size of a cantaloupe, has told me that I should not be sitting for long periods of time. He has given me new wee-wee pads that I'm still getting used to and, Dottie dear, you know, I would never forgive myself if I left a puddle on one of those nice silk sofa cushions of yours. But please include me in your next recital." The two thwarted musical divas are by this time beside themselves and race to bring their mess-terpiece to a triumphant crescendo. They come to the finale and stop as abruptly as they started, both panting and perspiring. There is a surprised moment of silence. "...Be of good cheer dear, and pray I pass a kidney stone." Click. A patter of polite applause follows. Dottie turns to me and asks, "Did somebody just call?"

The dynamic duo sip their ice water and briefly confer. "One more!" the brusque Bulgarian begrudgingly announces as though we had all leapt to our feet, tears streaming down our faces, begging for an encore. Mercy...I think to myself... if it weren't for the case of hysterical giggles I had gotten during Fanny's call, I would stick my finger in the electric wall socket about now just so the EMTs might roll me out of here on the next available gurney. But at least the good news is there's only one more of these to suffer through.

Suddenly, without warning, as is their way, the two attack their next ill-rehearsed piece of musical business. More random, off-key notes ring out. More accusing looks are bitterly exchanged between the two. Dottie leans into me and whispers, "Is it hot in here?" "A bit, yes" I answer. She nods... "I thought so, too." She quietly gets up and tiptoes over to a nearby wall switch and flips it. A ceiling fan, which is directly over the two musicians, comes dramatically to life, causing a white tornado of sheet music to be sucked up into the air. There is mass confusion as everyone dives after this flying sheet and that. During the melee, I grab the bottle of red back. Apparently, after tonight's fiasco, my moral compass is on the blink;

and I am willing to steal the wine out of an old lady's mouth. The musicians have thrown their hands up in the air. This is finally more than even they can bear. Dottie calls the room to attention. "Everyone, not to worry, we will reschedule with these two gifted virtuosos in the near future." There is subdued applause as people grab their coats and run for the door as though a fireman with a megaphone just yelled, "The house is on fire! Save yourselves!"

Lanier and I take the time to at least thank Dottie as the other attendees squeeze past. As I turn to go, she grabs my arm; I'm thinking she's going to ask for the wine back. Instead, she says, "This was such a success... you think I should charge admission for the next one?"

Definitely.

THE HAPPY WINO

When Black Friday hit Wall Street, it shook the walls of our 18th century coastal home worse than Hurricane Hugo. We were just recovering from a Writer's Strike and happily thinking that we were once more returning to our fantastical satirical animated series, 'Tripping the Rift' on the Sci-Fi Network; when they dropped the bomb on us that the series was being cancelled. The show was doing just great till they changed the lead-in show to our show and substituted a reality TV. turd, where two spooked nitwits ran around allegedly "haunted" houses, shrieking at shadowy corners. (Their sensitive equipment from Radio Shack supposedly registering unhappy spirit moans and groans. Maybe the ghosts were watching the show!) Their flimsy spook fest cost about two dollars to make; ours, which involved the combined hard work of a team of talented writers, animators and voice-over actors...quite a bit more. So we got the hook and the unemployment line and those two, no doubt, a beach house in Malibu with a hot tub. No hard feelings. Yeah right!!! And now... this Black Friday business. (As an aside, may I just say for the record that if I were black, I would most likely be quite offended that when something's bad; white people feel the need to put the word "black" in front of it. Ice is nice, but not "black ice"; that'll have you skidding off a cliff to your death. White sheep help you sleep but a "black sheep" is just a good-for-nothing wooly fuck-up. Why not call the Wall Street implosion..."White-Fright Friday"? Oh, never mind. Just file that under 'If I Ruled the World' and forget it...)

Luckily, President Obama soon announced that relief was on the way in the form of a "Loan Modification Program" that would easily allow us to significantly reduce our mortgage payment. It was to start immediately. The problem was someone apparently forgot to tell the Wells Fargo Bank brass. Whenever I called about it, one of their reps said things like, "We're still trying to figure out what that is." or "We're not exactly sure how it's going to work." "How 'bout I explain it to you?", I told whatever lame Wells Fargoan I got on the phone. "You reduce my mortgage payment like the government has already clearly spelled out and I keep my house." In response, I got a lot of confused mortgage mumbo-jumbo and a well-rehearsed polite promise to get back to me...someday. Sadly, as we all know, 'someday' is not a day of the week.

So that is how I came to take a job writing a wine column for the local paper, The Island News. Under my present dire circumstances, I needed more money and a lot more wine and whaddaya' know? All those frustrating years in Hollywood, guzzling all that great California grape juice, had accidentally turned me into somewhat of an expert on the stuff. I called my column, 'The Happy Wino' since, thanks to the good people at Wells Fargo, happy hour was now the only time of the day that I got any relief from wringing my hands with worry and pulling out my hair. My personal observations on wine drinking mixed with a smattering of viticulture struck an immediate chord in a town where drinking to excess was absolutely encouraged. After all, the town's founding charter had been signed in a tavern and it was here in Beaufort that the "pre-drink" was invented. That's when someone invites you to their house for a drink at five o'clock because the cocktail/dinner party you're both invited to doesn't start till six. Who can wait that long? Not a Southerner.

In the meantime, I also took a job at a fine-dining restaurant in town called Breakwater that had just relocated and undergone a classy renovation. I became its Wine Director and in keeping with my new position, dressed myself up in Gatsby-esque finery, which included a dashing collection of silk pocket squares that screamed, "this gentleman most certainly knows his way around a wine cellar." The truth was when snobby out-of-town strangers asked if I was a 'sommelier', it delighted me to inform them, "Actually, I'm 'some-old-gay' who just knows what he likes." I loved being a wine director. My afternoons were filled with vendors and wine reps peddling their wares. There were endless wine tastings with lots of swirling and sipping and spitting- well, lots of swirling and sipping not so much spitting if you get my drift. I couldn't believe I was actually getting paid to drink in the middle of the day. Why didn't I think of this career earlier? It was like winning the Irish Sweepstakes!

My wine column developed quite a following here in Beaufort perhaps because of its oh-so-honest take on wine's euphoric upside and often dizzying downside. Here's one to show you what I mean…

The Mean Glass

Oh the joy of wine! In its warm fuzzy afterglow, how different the world looks and sounds. Is that my neighbor's ear-shattering leaf blower I hear?! Not after several glasses of Louis Latour 2006 Vire Clesse. More like the gentle buzz of a thousand honey bees. What's that I see in my yard?! Did some trashy passerby toss his empty crushed Budweiser can into my azaleas? Another glass of my delicious Louis Latour and suddenly I see it more as a chic aluminum 'object-de-garden-art' by renowned German sculptor Anhauser Busch. And as for myself, all my flaws and imperfections seem to melt away (especially after several more snootfuls). It must be obvious to anyone with eyes, Monsieur Latour tells me, that I am at the 'top of my game', the 'peak of my intellectual powers' and the very embodiment of 'worldly wisdom'. Obvious to anyone but Lanier, who has the nerve to say to me: "You're slurring, I think you oughta slow down on the vino."

"WHAT?! What did you just shay?!" I ask, fuming with the kind of righteous overreaction that only a drunk can muster.

"I'm just saying I think you might wanna give it a rest," says Lanier, quietly.

Well, that timid suggestion is all it takes for the Mean Glass to come banging on my door, demanding satisfaction. "YOU KNOW

WHAT YOUR PROBLEM IS?" I hiss. "YOU'RE A CONTROL FREAK!" This to someone who, only minutes before, I saw as near to perfect as a human can be.

Ask any married couple, and they'll tell you. When the Mean Glass hits, RUN!! Sometimes it's you, sometimes it's them, and no one ever knows just what might set it off. Our friend Kathy reported to us one of her recent Mean Glass moments. She and her British husband were having a lovely evening, when he sweetly suggested that she "ease up on the Pinot Grigio." Her response? "YOU KNOW WHAT YOUR PROBLEM IS? YOU'RE ENGLISH! FUCK YOU AND FUCK YOUR COUNTRY!"

"Not exactly the high point of our marriage," says Kathy, sheepishly.

"YOU KNOW WHAT YOUR PROBLEM IS?!" remains the universal battle cry of the Mean Glass and is almost always followed by the nonsensical insult. Once when Lanier politely implied, after a boozy night out on the town, that I didn't really need to open a new bottle of wine at midnight, I aristocratically tossed out at him "YOU KNOW WHAT YOUR PROBLEM IS? YOU ARE SOOOO MIDDLE CLASS!" Totally overlooking the fact that I'm the son of a Long Island butcher and his Sicilian fishwife and Lanier's the direct descendant of Sir Nicholas Lanier, 'Master of the King's Music' to King Charles II.

The Mean Glass doesn't care whom it says what to. Basically its evil plan is to drive your loved one as far away as possible so the road is clear for a return trip to Wineville... without them sticking their big fat nose in your wine glass. But are you really mad at them? Nah. Deep down you know you love them and you feel safe enough to let off a little steam, saying to them what you couldn't say to your boss, your mother-in- law, that pain-in-the-butt client, or any number of petty tyrants who walk all over you and your world all day long. So next time when you gently ask your mate: "Don't you think you've had enough?" and they answer out of the blue: "LET'S GET A DIVORCE, SELL EVERYTHING AND SPLIT IT DOWN THE MIDDLE!"... know it's really just their way of saying: "I want another glass of wine" (no matter how many they've already had!)

The Mean Glass is, of course, not to be confused with The Horny Glass which usually hits one late in a raucous cocktail party or late night at a restaurant that's turned into a bar. Our friend Liza says she always knows when it hits because "I'm suddenly attracted to every man in the room EXCEPT my husband." Usually that leads to some guilty confession the next morning. "Honey, last night when I was out with the girls I ended up kissing some guy at the bar and I just wanted you to hear about it from me first. It meant absolutely nothing." And it didn't, because it wasn't really you. It was The Horny Glass that had momentarily taken possession of your lips. Blessedly, you often don't remember who or what the Horny Glass told you to do. Which means it doesn't count!

Not to be forgotten is The Weepy Glass, which can occur about 2 1/2 hours into a joy-filled wine party. When this strikes, it's best to just sneak away from the hapless 'Weepy Glass' victim as there is no amount of logic or common sense that will make this person stop crying. They just need to get that emotional lump out of their throat and will awake happy and refreshed in the morning without any help from you. Some people use the Weepy Glass as a way to deal with problems without paying a shrink. We all have that special tearjerker of a tune that we play over and over again once we've had the Weepy Glass (mine's 'Moon River'). My cousin Carol says she once woke up at dawn on the floor in front of her CD player with her arm outstretched and her finger still touching the button; she had obviously replayed Edith Piaf's 'La Vie En Rose' till she (ahem) 'fell asleep' next to her empty, overturned wine bottle. "It was humiliating, to say the least, but I'd finally cried my divorce out and felt better than I had in months!" confesses Carol. "And I don't even understand a word of French!"

So whether it's the bad boy Mean Glass, the oversexed Horny Glass, or the old self pitying 'swallow and wallow' Weepy Glass that decides to spend the night; just remember…they'll be gone and forgotten in the morning. Hopefully, most of all, by the person you may or may not still be married to.

Cheers!

Taking it on the Chin

I'm floating up Shit Creek and no… that's not a real creek down here. I have some serious money problems. I've been in a financial tug-of-war for over a year with the Wells Fargo Mortgage Company (who, by the way, now have me on their imaginary Loan Modification Waiting List… hardy har har.) The worst of it comes on December 1st, when I open my mailbox to find there's a letter from said company saying, "We have turned your loan over to the legal firm of Hatchetman, Meanburg, and McGreedy and they will begin foreclosure proceedings immediately. You have (30) days!" Beside myself, I call Wells Fargo to beg them to call off their dogs, but all of their lines are busy. So, sadly, I am put on hold with sappy holiday music. "I'll be home for Christmas", croons Michael Bublé wistfully in my ear. You might, Bublé, but not me. Thanks to Wells Fargo, on Christmas day, while I'm outside loading up a moving van, Hachetman, Meanburg, and McGreedy are going to be in *my* home drinking egg nog and reading the Wall Street Journal.

I quickly put my house on the market and next to the 'For Sale' sign, plant a Saint Joseph upside down (as is the superstition down here) to speed up the sale… while you're at it, Saint Joseph, get off your upside down ass and find me a buyer for my screenplay that's been languishing out in Hollywood for months without so much as a nibble. Oh, why did I ever leave Hollywood? Out of sight, out of mind. What was I thinking?! Never mind this wonderful life I have down here in Beaufort, South Carolina. Who needs a life? Maybe it'd be better to suck it up and get back in the game… Was it really that bad being in show business back in L.A.? Was it?

As if Hollywood itself had heard me, a phone call comes a week later, from an actor/producer friend of a friend who, unbeknownst to me, has shown my script to a mysterious and powerful Hong Kong investor named Mr. Chin who loves the movie and "wants to make it happen". I immediately agree to do a conference call with him, although I can't even imagine why someone from China would be interested in an outrageous spoof of C.S.I. called D.U.M.I. ('Detroit Unsolved Morgue Investigations')? Has the average Chinese man on the street ever even heard of Detroit?

Who cares? I can't think about that. I've got a historic house heading for the auction block. So I busily ready myself to negotiate with this Chinese Dragon minus my fakey love-you-babe agent who dropped me the minute I moved out of L.A. I'm nerved up and anxious about the call, but at least I'll have my co-writers, Lanier and Mark Amato, on it with me. No…as fate would have it, neither one can do the call, so I face the formidable Mr. Chin…alone (gulp). That is, except for the inexperienced novice actor-turned-producer back in L.A. who will be on the other line of the conference call with me. Unfortunately, I can already hear him heavy breathing nervously into his cell phone. Great.

"Mr. Chin… you're on with Terry Sweeney… the other two writers were regrettably… unavailable. Sorry." Mr. Chin sternly addresses me, "Okay…Terry Sweeney… you will repeat all I say to udder writers. Yes?" "Yes!!" I stammer back. Then, trying to make small talk, he goes on about a house he has in 'Maraboo' and his udder house in 'Connericut'. At least that's what it sounded like he said. His accent is so thick I can barely understand a word he says. I wing it and coo back fawningly, "Yes, both beautiful places to live." Then he rambles on about some other something or other he owns in China that, for the life of me, I can't decipher…it could be anything from a sesame noodle factory to a girl baby chop shop. I haven't a clue. But he laughs so I laugh too…too long and too loud. Mercifully, he gets to the purpose of his call.

His tone suddenly changes to one of mocking sarcasm, "Let me ask you something, Terry Sweeney…are you the kind of writer whose script is your *baby* and nobody can touch your *baby* because you *artist* and dis some great work of *art* with your heart and soul in every line? You dat kind of writer?" (As a matter of fact…yes…I think to myself; that's why I chose to make it my life's work.) But from his humiliating tone of voice, I can tell that's not the answer Moneybags wants to hear… and so I answer calmly, "Not at all." Then trying to hide any hints of 'artistic temperament', I finish with "I welcome feedback and try to remain open to any and all suggestions that will make the script better." "Good!" he barks back, "Right answer! So I give you changes, you take?" Take changes? I've got lowdown dirty crooks from Wells Fargo counting the days until they confiscate my house keys. "Yes! I take!" I take?! I even sound vaguely Asian at this point. Next, I'll be bowing and wearing kabuki make-up and a kimono.

In a quiet, intense voice, he continues, "Let me tell you something, Terry Sweeney…" (Then suddenly yelling)…"I NO GIVE FUCKING SHIT ABOUT PLOT! NO GIVE FUCKING SHIT ABOUT PLOT!!! MOVIE GOTTA MAKE MONEY!– Oh, sorry, I say 'fucking shit' so much. I work on floor of Hong Kong Stock Exchange many year, and it 'fucking shit dis' and 'fucking shit dat', so I will try not to say 'fucking shit' rest of talk." "Thank you, Mr. Chin. But I've heard that sort of language before." I demurely toss back, trying to play the easiest person in the free world you could ever hope to work with. He's oblivious. "I show your script, Terry Sweeney, to focus groups." He what?! He'd usually have to sign a confidentially agreement to read it himself! My mind is racing. How many millions of Chinese have read my movie script? For all I know, it's being shot now and factories in Hong Kong are prepping hats, tee shirts, and… and… vibrators with my movie's 'D.U.M.I.' logo plastered on them to accompany its market launch. Flabbergasted, I say nothing and let him continue. "Results will surprise you, Terry Sweeney." He goes on sounding very surprised himself, "Sophisticated people like your movie…professional women like your movie… investment bankers like your movie." "Yes, well… that's who I wrote it for…investment bankers." I offer up shakily. Hint. Hint. "People who I represent have lotta money but no have talent. No can write funny movie like you." "Well, I have a lotta talent but no money. Sounds like a match made in Heaven!" I say, lightly tee-heeing. "NOT SO FAST!" yells Mr. Chin. "Something you must know about people I work for…" he adds ominously.

I don't know and I don't wanna know. Chinese mafia? Money launderers? Interpol's Most Wanted? Just write me a check. Check no bounce. Me happy. Mr. Chin continues on "You know how cheap Scotch person is… they so cheap only have bagpipe and wear skirt so not have to buy pants." I try to interrupt. "Are your business contacts, Scottish?" "No!" he answers sharply. "But you know who cheaper than Scotch person?" "I give up." I answer, knowing this is definitely a rhetorical question. "Jew!" he says, "Jew …cheap… cheap…cheap!!! Bet you think nobody cheaper than Jew." This fool doesn't even know if *I'm* Jewish. But hold on, my Hebrew friends;

good news is on the way. Mr. Chin is only too happy to enlighten me. "Cheaper than Jew… Dutch person!! You know how you go to restaurant and when bill come, you pay for yourself and nobody else… they say you go 'Dutch'. Dat cause Dutch people cheapest people in the world. And dat who I work for… International Investment Firm from Nederlands!"

Why do I have that sinking feeling that it's not going to be all warm and fuzzy tiptoeing through the tulips with my new tight-fisted Dutch friends? I bravely cut to the chase. "So, how much money are they willing to pay to option the script?" I am now very direct and no nonsense. I have nothing to lose… except the roof over my head. Let's hear it… "They no put money in until you have big star agree to be in movie!" says Mr. Chin grandly. "That need to be icing on cake for dem to take piece!" Oh, really? This movie is a satirical ensemble send-up, like a 'Naked Gun' or 'Scary Movie'. It is not based on a New York Times bestseller; nor does it have Academy Award written all over it or for that matter… anywhere near it. I start to try to explain this to Mr. Chin, but he cuts me off with a loud "LET ME KNOW WHO YOU GET, TERRY SWEENEY!!!" Click. I am reminded of that familiar Chinese food conundrum. I'm full but I'm still starving. The actor/producer guy is now silent on the other line. He's thinking, I guess. I'm kind of hoping for some post-traumatic conference call camaraderie. I wait a minute or two… nothing. "Uhh…Brad? Still there?" Suddenly, a desperate torrent of hysterical strategizing comes pouring out of him. "We can get somebody. I know people. We can find a star…some big star that's doing nothing but sitting on their ass. Sure. That's nothing. I can come up with a star. What about you?!?! You must know a star!!! THINK! THINK!" "Ok… uh…Star Jones?" I say, desperate to make light of our hopeless situation. "Asshole!" He screams and hangs up. I'm left holding the phone and staring at it.

Well. That was certainly *not* the exchange to get me packing my bags and taking off for them there Hollywood Hills. Instead, I head off to my wine rack. I need an appointment with Dr. Red Wine a.s.a.p. I pour the world's biggest glass and pad barefoot out to the old porch swing on my big white-columned veranda. I survey the lovely beautiful front lawn of 'Bythewood' (soon to be 'Wellsfargowood'). I lift my glass and give a wistful nod to St. Joseph. "It's down to you, Joe."

A week later, some wonderful local people from across the bridge offer to buy our house and miraculously, it closes quickly before the Four Wells Fargo Horsemen of the Apocalypse can gallop through the gates. As I pack up to leave, I find a lot of memorabilia in boxes from my past life in Hollywood. Lots of old copies of Hollywood Reporter and Variety. I wonder if one day, I will pass a newsstand and see a Variety with my movie, 'D.U.M.I.' splashed across the front page touted as China's biggest box office hit with one small change; it's now called B.U.M.I. – Beijing Unsolved Morgue Investigations.

I don't care. This afternoon, the sun is magically lighting up the Spanish moss and a nearby magnolia's giant blooms are wafting their delicate scent in through an open window. Luckily, sweet Lanier and I have already found an adorable historic cottage to rent. I've definitely decided I'm going to try and make it work down here. I have love and laughter. I have good friends by the dozens, and I have the promise of new adventures and a new life. The South has helped me rise again… and I will forever be grateful to Her.

ABOUT THE AUTHOR

Terry Sweeney graduated from Middlebury College where he studied creative writing. After moving back to his native New York, he was hired as a writer for Saturday Night Live. He also co-wrote the screenplay for the cult Southern film 'Shag' which was recently chosen by Garden and Gun Magazine as one of The Souths Ten Greatest Films. Sweeney later joined the cast of Saturday Night Live in the 80's and there, became famous for imitating First Lady Nancy Reagan, and also made history as the first openly gay performer on American television. After SNL he continued to write screenplays and television in Hollywood. This first collection of autobiographical essays marks his return to his literary roots. Sweeney lives with his husband Lanier Laney in a historic cottage in Beaufort SC.